Educational Leadership and Technology

Providing models of exemplary use and the latest research, *Educational Leadership and Technology* reveals the transformational power of emerging technologies to improve student learning and explores how leaders can bring about this technology integration. This book provides an overview of roles and strategies expected of effective school leaders, as well as some of the complex issues they face. Authors Garland and Tadeja offer a critical analysis of today's emerging technology, while also addressing the need for collaborative efforts of parents, community, and students to implement technologies effectively.

Special features include:

- Full integration of National Technology Standards for Administrators (NETS.A) and the National Education Technology Plan (NETP).
- Leader reflections from practicing school administrators that provide context of real-world scenarios.
- "Tips for School Leaders" and end-of-chapter questions that encourage student engagement with the text.
- "School Administrator's Technology Leadership Self-Assessment," a unique and impartial survey in each chapter with self-scoring guide that helps readers determine their technology use and readiness for implementation.
- A robust companion website with PowerPoint Slides, strategies, and links to website and video resources which will reflect changes in technology, policy, and practice.
- Discussion of the newest and emerging technologies, including Cloudware, social media, virtual manipulatives, and e-games.

Educational Leadership and Technology is an important resource for new and aspiring elementary, middle, and high school principals as well as superintendents and technology coordinators.

Virginia E. Garland is Associate Professor of Education at the University of New Hampshire, USA.

Chester Tadeja is Adjunct Professor in Education at the University of La Verne, USA.

Educational Leadership and Technology

Preparing School Administrators for a Digital Age

VIRGINIA E. GARLAND AND CHESTER TADEJA

Routledge
Taylor & Francis Group

NEW YORK AND LONDON

First published 2013
by Routledge
711 Third Avenue, New York, NY 10017

Simultaneously published in the UK
by Routledge
2 Park Square, Milton Park, Abingdon, Oxon OX14 4RN

Routledge is an imprint of the Taylor & Francis Group, an informa business

Library of Congress Cataloging in Publication Data
Garland, Virginia E.
Educational leadership and technology : preparing school administrators for a digital age / by Virginia E. Garland and Chester Tadeja.
    p. cm.
  Includes bibliographical references and index.
  1. Educational leadership—United States.   2. School administrators—Effect of technological innovations on.   3. Educational technology—United States.
  I. Tadeja, Chester.   II. Title.
  LB2805.G29 2013
  371.2—dc23
  2012026901

ISBN: 978-0-415-80976-4 (hbk)
ISBN: 978-0-415-80978-8 (pbk)
ISBN: 978-0-203-13470-2 (ebk)

Typeset in Sabon and Helvetica Neue
by RefineCatch Limited, Bungay, Suffolk

SUSTAINABLE FORESTRY INITIATIVE

Certified Sourcing
www.sfiprogram.org
SFI-00555
The SFI label applies to the text stock.

Printed and bound in the United States of America by
Walsworth Publishing Company, Marceline, MO.

Dedication

For the New Hampshire Society for the Prevention of Cruelty to Animals and its online support of companion animal adoptions.
V. G.

For my loving wife, Christina: For your unwavering support and encouragement. I love you.
C. T.

Contents

Detailed Contents

Preface

Welcome to *Educational Leadership and Technology: Preparing School Administrators for a Digital Age*. This textbook, along with its companion website and resources, is written for pre-service and in-service school administrators and technology coordinators. The focus of the book is on how to harness the transformational power of emerging technologies for improving student learning.

There is a great need for effective technology-driven instruction. American schools are encountering poor student performance, high dropout rates and waning world leader status in education. In order to address those challenges, national and international policy initiatives recently emerged as catalysts for changing the professional practices of educational leaders across the globe. In 2009, the International Society for Technology in Education (ISTE) revised the five National Educational Technology Standards and Performance Indicators for Administrators (NETS.A). A year later, in 2010, the Office of Educational Technology of the United States Department of Education published *Transforming American Education: Learning Powered by Technology*, also known as the National Education Technology Plan (NETP). This book examines both the five NETS.A standards and the different, but similar, five NETP goals.

School principals, district superintendents, and technology coordinators are increasingly evaluated by performance criteria, which include some or all of the NETS.A standards. School districts across the nation have been using the refreshed 2009 ISTE NETS.A five standards to assess the effectiveness of building and district-level administrators (National Educational Technology Standards for Administrators, 2009). There are indications that most school leaders are deficient in at least one area. The NETP goals are also becoming benchmarks for effective school district operations and technology planning. This textbook will assist school leaders in overcoming challenges in order to meet these standards and goals.

Educational Leadership and Technology: Preparing School Administrators for a Digital Age provides both critical analysis and practical advice for educators, professors, and practitioners alike on examining and implementing the technology standards and the national education goals. In 2010, due in part to poor performance by American students on international assessments, the United States Secretary of Education led a panel of experts and the Office of Educational Technology, with considerable public input, to develop the National Education Technology Plan, *Transforming American*

Education: Learning Powered by Technology (Transforming American Education, 2010). The plan is not without its critics. Some educational leaders, including ISTE's chief executive officer, complain that there is a lack of funding for the current NETP program (Herbert, 2010).

The textbook pays careful attention to the leadership roles played by school leaders in bringing about the kind of digital age technology integration encouraged by the NETP goals and the NETS.A standards.

Pioneering these kinds of changes in the professional practice of school administrators requires a better understanding of the emerging technologies of today while offering different approaches to facilitate systemic growth. This book gives an overview of topics, issues, and strategies aimed at incorporating diverse perspectives within leadership and supervisory practices of the school building and district-level leader. Professional development is a growing constant in educational circles. With the emergence and proliferation of the Internet, technology now takes center stage in how learning communities get together to share information on best practices and to incorporate the teaching and learning process to better help students succeed. This book equips school leaders, digital natives, and digital immigrants alike to collaborate for systemic change. It is also a useful tool for professors of education administration because it combines recent scholarship and practical strategies. The reflections from leaders across the country, the case studies, the tips for leaders, and the surveys are just some of the ways in which the readers can become engaged in the transformational powers of technology in education.

Organization of the Book

This textbook is organized according to new national goals and international standards for technology in schools. The five NETS.A standards expected of effective school principals, program directors, technology coordinators, and superintendents are closely aligned to this book's six chapters: technology planning; leading instruction; teacher supervision and professional development; technology infrastructure; systemic change in technology; and legal and social issues in technology. The five NETP goals are also addressed in several chapters, especially those in which the impact of new technologies upon learning, assessment, teaching, infrastructure, and productivity is investigated. Thus, the six chapters are vibrantly connected to not only the latest in research but also to emerging educational technology trends, including the use of social networking tools in both instruction and teacher supervision.

Each of the six chapters of the book includes the following sections:

■ synopsis of the cases, goals, and standards;

■ leader(s') reflection(s) from practicing school administrator(s) or technology coordinator(s) from Maine to California;

■ introduction to the topic;

■ tables of NETP goals and/or NETS.A standards;

■ recent research on emerging educational technology trends;

- implementation strategies and effective practice;

- tips for school leaders;

- summary;

- School Administrator's Technology Leadership Self-Assessment Survey;

- discussion questions;

- PowerPoint slides of topics in the chapter (which can be found on the companion website).

References and website resources are at the end of the book.

Special Features

Educational Leadership and Technology: Preparing School Administrators for a Digital Age has several special features not found in any other textbook. Whereas some books have addressed the NETS.A standards, in this textbook the authors align both the refreshed International Society of Technology in Education's 2009 National Education Technology Standards for Administrators with the newer 2010 National Educational Technology Plan's goals. This broader and more substantive approach to currently used technology standards ensures more effective implementation strategies for building and district-level school administrators and technology coordinators.

Another unique aspect of this book is its analysis of emerging technologies, such as cloudware, social media, simulations, and other real-time collaboration tools and their impact in an ever-flattening digital world. The digital immigrant and digital native users are types of today's technology learners. How does this play out at the global level? How can a pre-service in-service administrator harness the power of both? These critical issues are addressed in reflections from leaders across the nation, another special feature of this book. Other emerging technologies that are both relevant and necessary for discussion include the use of virtual manipulatives, global learning, storytelling, multimedia, virtual schooling, e-books and e-games, auditory learning, the future textbook, and efficient assessments. The authors provide real-life scenarios and tools to help address each topic, including the "Tips for School Leaders" section in each chapter. This added value lends itself to maximizing efficiency in the role of the school leader, who is more accountable than ever!

Perhaps the most valuable special feature of this text is the School Administrator's Technology Leadership Self-Assessment. It is a unique and impartial survey that reflects the specific goals and standards presented in each of the six chapters of the book. Readers should use it to better determine their technology use and preparedness for implementation in their schools and districts. The authors offer a self-scoring survey for the respondents to complete. School administrators who rate themselves and their schools or districts with scores of 5 and 4 are already meeting the standards indicated in those items. Ratings of 1 or 2 would indicate areas of needed professional growth by either the school district, or the school leader, or both in order to meet the NETS.A standards or NETP goals. This instrument is a useful pre-assessment tool for instructors or professional development facilitators who are using the book. Low ratings would indicate areas where readers need additional attention. For example, if graduate students or workshop participants indicate that either they or their school districts do not use electronic portfolios of student work effectively, then they will want to explore additional resources and professional development on that topic.

The School Administrator's Technology Leadership Self-Assessment results can also be used to create an individualized e-portfolio. More commonly used by students and teachers to collect digital work of educational progress and achievements, e-portfolios can be used by school leaders to "communicate the progress of your school by documenting the success of programs the reader has initiated, and they are a great way to manage all the documents involved in your school's review and accreditation process" (Schrum and Levin, 2009, pp. 133–134). There are free Web 2.0 tools and a useful website (http://electronicportfolios.org) for e-portfolio creation.

In addition, the authors hope that the instructor or the professional development facilitator will find a supplemental companion website to the text helpful in designing class or workshop activities. The companion website includes not only PowerPoint slides for each chapter, but also helpful website resources for elementary, middle and high school principals, as well as superintendents and technology coordinators.

Acknowledgments

The authors are indebted to several individuals who helped us with this textbook. Our Routledge editor, Heather Jarrow, patiently supported us and gave us insights on ways to improve our writing. We are also thankful to those educational leaders who so kindly and expertly provided us with the thoughtful leader reflections for each chapter: Judith Arrow, Bill Carozza, Steve Chamberlin, Karen Connaghan, Greg DeYoung, Jill Hobson, Andy Korman, Steve Mashburn, and John David Son.

Virginia E. Garland
University of New Hampshire

Chester Tadeja
Pomona Unified School District, California

Acronyms and Abbreviations

AASL	American Association of School Librarians
AMS	Assessment Management Systems
AP	advanced placement
AUP	acceptable use policy
AYP	adequate yearly progress
BYOT	Bring Your Own Technology
CDS	Common Data Standards
CIPA	Children's Internet Protection Act
EG	Entertainment Gathering conference
ELL	English language learner
EMIS	Education Management Information System
FCC	Federal Communications Commission
FERPA	Family Educational Rights and Privacy Act
GEL	Good Experience Live conference
GPS	Global Positioning Systems
ICT	information and communication technology
IEP	Individualized Education Plan
ISTE	International Society for Technology in Education
IT	information technology
KIPP	Knowledge is Power Program
LMS	Learning Management System
MIS	management information systems
NCLB	No Child Left Behind Act
NETP	National Education Technology Plan
NETS.A	National Educational Technology Standards and Performance Indicators for Administrators
NETS.S	National Educational Technology Standards for Students
NSF	National Science Foundation
OER	open educational resource
OSI	Open Source Initiative
PA	public address
PADI	Principled-Assessment Designs for Inquiry
PLC	Professional Learning Community
QR	Quick Response
SaaS	Software as a Service

SHEEO	State Higher Education Executive Officers
STEM	science, technology, engineering, and mathematics
TED	Technology, Entertainment, Design conference
UDL	Universal Design for Learning
UUPP	Urban Universities Portfolio Project
VLACS	Virtual Learning Academy Charter School

1
Technology Planning

Synopsis

The conceptual framework of this book is introduced in the Preface. The International Society for Technology in Education (ISTE) revamped its five technology standards for school administrators (NETS.A) in 2009. Then, the Office of Educational Technology of the United States Department of Education published *Transforming American Education: Learning Powered by Technology*, also known as the National Education Technology Plan (NETP), during late 2010. In the years since the policy initiatives were established, newer technology tools have emerged. This textbook examines how skilled leaders in select schools throughout the country have used digital tools to improve instruction and student learning.

In Chapter 1, solution strategies are given for effective implementation of the first NETS.A standard of having visionary leadership in technology planning and the NETP goal of improving American schools' productivity. An overview of the leadership skills needed to implement this common core of standards (NETS.A) and goals (NETP) is supplemented by practical advice for school leaders of all grade levels. The roles of principals, program directors, technology coordinators, curriculum coordinators, and superintendents as leaders and implementers of emerging technologies are discussed. Recent research is presented as part of an analysis of the technology-adept school leader as visionary, as data-driven decision-maker, and as change agent. Strategies for developing effective technology plans and strategic plans include suggestions for stake-holder roles, for transitioning from mission statement to planning, and for fostering innovation. A sample technology plan mission statement for the Pomona Unified School District in California is provided. The reader's responses to a self-assessment survey for Chapter 1 will assist the educational leader in achieving effective technology plan implementation on both the building and district levels. The leader's reflection at the beginning of this chapter provides a realistic scenario of the challenges involved in designing and implementing a school district technology plan.

References are provided at the end of the book and web-based resources are provided on a companion website to further assist the school leader in developing his or her action plan, which could take the form of an e-portfolio. The reader and the professor, instructor, or professional development workshop leader who are using this text might also find the companion website's resources and PowerPoint slides for Chapter 1 of use in understanding its theme of technology planning in the digital age.

Reflections of an Assistant Superintendent in California

Tech plans will change over the years. One of the most important aspects that organizations need to understand in determining their tech plan is to be aware of the elements that will be included in the tech plan itself. This may sound like reasonable advice. But consider that as our district began to look at our own tech plans, the county began to change the recommendations and requirements of the written tech plan and we had to rewrite ours in the middle of the year! The first thing is to go to an expert who knows the requirements. There are different funds that go in to the making of a tech plan. If a smaller district writes a 50-page tech plan, for instance, and ends up getting a smaller amount, then it's best to understand what you are going to get from it. Writing a tech plan is very complicated so you'll need to contact someone from the state or someone from the county office to move this along.

I just don't think it's wise to simply write a tech plan. We need to go in and say what is this a requirement for? This will determine what angle you'll put on it. The U.S. Department of Education is working on strengthening things they will offer and things they will cut, so you really need to understand why you are writing it. This may be a complicated way to start, but you don't want to start on your tech plan and realize you don't need a big curriculum piece or a large budget piece. Unfortunately, all states are different; but it's best to have as many advocates on your side. I think people don't start there, however. I've seen individuals just start writing the plan. They need to be more aware of why they're writing it and what it's going to get them or what it's not going to get them.

It's also important to have all stakeholders at the beginning of the process when starting your tech plan. That should include someone at the district level, site level and include a teacher and a curriculum designer. Technical aspects are going to be just as important as curriculum. These two things need to bridge.

Finally, a self-evaluation of what is already in place is necessary. The idea of iPads may be nice for every student. But this may not necessarily serve the needs of the students very well, but a different need altogether. So a needs assessment is critical. The biggest premise of the tech plan, and what we may have lost sight of a little bit, is that it must be for learning. Just having a laptop for very child may look good; but answering the question of what do we want students to learn is even more important.

Judith Arrow is the director of educational services at Dixie School District and is the assistant superintendent of educational services of the Marin County Office of Education, approximately 20 miles north of San Francisco. In this capacity, she oversees all technology plans written in Marin County, ultimately serving over 30,000 students. The Dixie Elementary School is a National Blue Ribbon School and a California Distinguished School.

Introduction

What makes an administrator ready for the digital age? What kinds of leadership skills are necessary for both in-service and pre-service administrators to lead in today's ever-changing field of technology? Both the NETP goals and the NETS.A standards clearly mandate new roles for educational leaders as both visionaries and strategic planners in the implementation of technology-powered learning opportunities for students (Brooks-Young, 2009; Williamson and Redish, 2009). Transformational leadership is needed to infuse emerging technologies (Garland, 2010a; Picciano, 2011; Tadeja, 2011b) in the key functions of educational administrators: planning, communicating, and advocating for cost effective technology implementation in curriculum and instruction, assessment, and professional development.

In order to lead and collaborate effectively with other educators and policy-makers in the digital age, educational administrators need to take full advantage of the wireless revolution and its impact upon the infrastructure of school districts. According to the U.S. Department of Education's National Education Technology Plan authors: "This revolutionary opportunity for change is driven by the continuing push of emerging technology and the pull of the critical national need for new strategies to turn around a P-12 system that is failing to adequately prepare young Americans for postsecondary education and the workforce" (U.S. Department of Education, 2010, p. 52).

Transforming Productivity

In the fifth goal of the National Education Technology Plan, "Productivity: Redesign and Transform," some of the current challenges to improving student learning are addressed. In order to accomplish the transformation of American education, school leaders must recognize and use the "power of technology" to improve student productivity, while making "more efficient use of time, money, and staff" (NETP Goal 5.0). Defining productivity, rethinking traditional assumptions about schooling, developing useful metrics, and ensuring student progress to graduation are basic to improving student productivity (O'Neil and Perez, 2002; Schrum and Levin, 2009).

Here are the major components, as outlined by the blue panel of experts of NETP's Goal 5: "Productivity: Redesign and Transform":

> 5.0 Productivity: Our education system at all levels will redesign processes and structures to take advantage of the power of technology to improve learning outcomes while making more efficient use of time, money, and staff. To meet this goal, we recommend the following actions:

> 5.1 Develop and adopt a common definition of productivity in education and more relevant and meaningful measures of outcomes, along with improved policies and technologies for managing costs, including those for procurement [. . .]

> 5.2 Rethink basic assumptions in our education system that inhibit leveraging technology to improve learning, starting with our current practice

of organizing student and educator learning around seat time instead of the demonstration of competencies [. . .]

5.3 Develop useful metrics for the educational use of technology in states and districts [. . .]

5.4 Design, implement, and evaluate technology-powered programs and interventions to ensure that students progress seamlessly through our P-16 education system and emerge prepared for college and careers [. . .].
(U.S. Department of Education, 2010, pp. 73–74).

By a common definition of productivity (NETP Goal 5.1), the technology plan authors mean that there should be a consensus among school district leaders on "meaningful measures of outcomes" and procurement costs. The specific goal of NETP 5.1 is to track the "ratio of outcomes to costs." Although this is a common business practice, it is difficult, at best, for educators to meaningfully measure what students have learned. Although there are standardized tests, many educational researchers maintain that those assess-ments do not adequately measure what students know (Reeves, 2007). The affective dimension is overlooked. The valuable concept of multiple intelligences is denied in the heavy reliance on only verbal or mathematical skills in standardized state or national tests. Analysis of student assessments is given more depth in the next chapter.

However, procurement costs can be made more streamlined with improved technology links between schools and suppliers. Purchase orders and the bidding process can be rendered more effective with the use of advances in data storage and analysis software packages.

Technology Enhanced Alternatives to Traditional Schools

NETP Goal 5.2 is the recognition that traditional forms of schooling have failed our students. Disengaged students are dropping out of school and performing poorly on international and state tests. This goal is a call for eliminating "seat time, organization of students into age-determined groups, the structure of separate academic disciplines, the organization of learning into classes of roughly equal size, and the use of time blocks" (U.S. Department of Education, 2010, p. 73). Virtual schooling, based on competency-based instruction, is one alternative proposed by NETP. Competency-based instruction, in which learners earn credit for mastery of skills and knowledge rather than for seat time in traditional teacher-led courses, is now policy for secondary-level students in some states. One model program is New Hampshire, where high school students earn graduation credit by demonstrating competence on state and local standards. New Hampshire school districts are now redesigning secondary-level courses to be competency based, with "authentic" or performance assessments of student work. According to Wolk (2007, p 54), with competency-based instruction, "Teachers and administrators will have to reinvent themselves, to put aside old conceptions and practices, and do something new and different. And there are other obstacles, like costs, No Child Left Behind, and college admissions standards." Despite these challenges, competency-based instruction has lowered the dropout rate and better prepared students for college, two essential goals of the National Education Technology Plan.

Extended learning time, such as the recent Massachusetts initiative to add instructional hours to schools in low-income areas, is a way to flexibly schedule learning time for students. Another school reform plan, the Knowledge is Power Program (KIPP), provides learning opportunities for at-risk, urban middle-school students in an extended school day. The KIPP advocates have embraced an extended learning time system that stems from their beliefs that the school day is too short. The traditional 180-day, 5-day week and the truncated schedule that many money-strapped school districts now face do not provide enough time for student learning. Dave Levin, co-founder of the KIPP school system, promotes a school day that starts at 7:30 a.m. and ends at 5 p.m. every week day, with Saturday school mandated twice a month and summer school required for at least three weeks. This program, which follows a charter system operation, was started in 1994 in Houston, Texas, and has grown to 109 KIPP schools in 20 states, serving more than 33,000 students. The curriculum is the same as the mandated federal curriculum standards, with each school operating autonomously. However, the academic achievement results that KIPP produces have been remarkable. In 2007, for instance, the KIPP school system commissioned the Mathematica Policy Research Institution to conduct a multi-year longitudinal study, which found that at least 94% of all KIPP eighth-grade students had outperformed their peers in non-KIPP programs in reading and math. Above average scores were reported in San Francisco, Denver, Baltimore, and other KIPP schools across the country. Another group of educational researchers found that KIPP students in one middle school achieved higher scores on four out of six standardized tests, compared with non-KIPP students in the same "large, high-poverty urban district" (Ross et al., 2007, p. 137).

The competency and online approaches to education can be facilitated by the use of technology and metrics (NETP Goal 5.3). A common practice in school districts is to collect data on numbers and types of computers and Internet connections; but data is really needed on how technology is used to support learning. Although almost all classrooms in public schools in the United States have Internet access, "many studies have demonstrated that computers are still found in computer labs, with limited access for integrated instructional uses, and students use technology far more outside of school than within the school environment, where it is often still seen as an 'addition' rather than a part of the curriculum" (Schrum and Levin, 2009, pp. 65–66). Analysis of what constitutes effective use of technology for learning is explored in the next chapter.

New Hampshire's recent educational reforms, including competency-based instruction and raising the dropout age from 16 to 18, are focused on ensuring that all students graduate from high school. According to the national technology plan authors, "technology-powered programs and interventions" (NETP Goal 5.4) should be used to reduce the dropout rate and more adequately prepare high school students for college. Data collection of student records and test results should be done "seamlessly through our P-16 education system." Chapter 2 deals with assessment data in more depth.

Visionary Leadership

The redesigned productivity (NETP 5) goal of the national technology plan can be achieved by means of the visionary leadership of educational administrators (NETS.A Standard 1). The first standard of the National Educational Technology Standards and

Performance Indicators for Administrators is on organizational change through shared technology planning.

Here are the key components of the International Society of Technology in Education's first standard of NETS.A, "Visionary Leadership":

> Educational Administrators inspire and lead development and implementation of a shared vision for comprehensive integration of technology to promote excellence and support transformation throughout the organization.
>
> Educational Administrators:
>
> (a) inspire and facilitate among all stakeholders a shared vision of purposeful change that maximizes use of digital-age resources to meet and exceed learning goals, support effective instructional practice, and maximize performance of district and school leaders;
>
> (b) engage in an ongoing process to develop, implement, and communicate technology-infused strategic plans aligned with a shared vision;
>
> (c) advocate on local, state, and national levels for policies, programs, and funding to support implementation of a technology-infused vision and strategic plan.
>
> (ISTE, 2009, p. 11)

The focus on collaboration between school administrators and teachers and other educational specialists cannot be understated. In their study of effective schools (those that had both high student achievement levels and Communities of Learners), DuFour and his co-authors found that all educators "worked collaboratively rather than in isolation. They developed common assessments and applied consistent standards rather than acting autonomously. They changed instructional pacing and strategies based on new insights into pedagogical effectiveness" (DuFour, et al., 2010, p183). The NETS.A first goal of a "shared vision" for "excellence" can be attained by involving all stakeholders in the planning process.

Goals of Technology Planning in Education

The principal, technology coordinator, and superintendent are urged to collaborate with key stakeholders, such as teachers, students, program and curriculum directors, parents, community members, and governmental officials, in strategic planning initiatives that enhance the most effective technology use in education (NETS.A Standard 1.a). Educational leaders are urged to use "digital-age resources" to meet student achievement targets, to support teachers in instructional practices which use technology tools, and to enhance their own professional practice. The instructional support area is key to Ormiston: "The general message of NETS for administrators is that leadership needs to model the use of Web 2.0 tools and to support teachers as they are learning to make technology integral in teaching and learning" (Ormiston, 2011, p. 95). Other educational researchers agree with Ormiston's views that school leaders must focus on technology integration in teaching because less than one third of teachers are using technology in their daily instruction, yet the underperforming "iGeneration" can be highly motivated by the digital tools that they are already using for social purposes (Ferriter and Garry, 2010). However, the number of Web 2.0 tools out there today far exceeds those being used in instruction. Chapter 2 describes the latest in technology tools for instruction and assessment, and Chapter 3 addresses professional development for school teachers and leaders alike.

The School District's Mission Statement

Strategic planning is a necessary skill of educational administrators in the digital age (NETS.A 1.b). School mission statements are part of a shared vision, and one that is developed by key stakeholders and communicated to the entire educational community, including students, parents, teachers, and other leaders and staff members. According to Brooks-Young (2009, p. 24), "research on effective schools supports the strategic planning model by finding that a critical element in school restructuring is the ability of school administrators to articulate the mission of the school and establish a focus that unifies the staff."

The Pomona (California) Unified School District Technology Use Plan is a model technology plan because it starts with a mission statement that is both visionary and strategic:

> The Pomona Unified School District is committed to providing opportunities for all students to develop their abilities and talents to the fullest extent possible. Participation in the global community demands that all educators and students be prepared to use technology well. The District will support instruction and enhance learning by helping teachers and students to integrate technology into the core curriculum in order to provide quality education and challenge students to reach their highest potential.
> (Pomona Unified School District Technology Use Plan, 2010)

The 69-page Pomona Unified School District Technology Use Plan (http://www.pusd. org/education/components/docmgr/default.php?sectiondetailid=1245&fileitem=561) provides a structured three-year plan to serve over 30,000 students in one of the largest K-12 districts in the state of California. It effectively uses technology resources to address two key issues in the district: high rates of poverty and English language learners (ELLs). Pomona Unified is a medium-sized school district and sits on the eastern edge of Los Angeles County. The district employs nearly 3,000 employees and services nearly 30,000 students. Approximately 85% of the student population is Hispanic/Latino. The city of Pomona is known for its low socio-economic status as high numbers of families receive state aid and many children in the student population receive free or reduced lunch.

Much of what was written in the Pomona Unified District mission statement encompasses four central concepts: respect, relationships, responsibility, and results. This theme-based moniker appears in every possible way around the district, including its website, letterhead, and official district memos. It also appears in nearly every speech by the superintendent or district officials. This type of theme is also embraced in the visionary roles that its leaders play. The theme focuses on a way of thinking and what both leaders and teachers are committed to doing:

- Respect: Where all stakeholders are valued partners.

- Relationships: Where genuine and caring connections are built.

- Responsibility: Where everyone is accountable.

- Results: That are reflected in a high level of student achievement.

The technology plan at Pomona Unified is a reflection of the mission statement goals because it revolves around the notions that students will respect themselves without cyber bullying, that students will build relationships with one another that are safe online practices, that students will be responsible in their own use of social networking tools in learning, and that teachers will practice legal and safe Internet practices while driving academic results. The Pomona technology plan comprises numerous factors, including as many stakeholders as possible. Students, teachers, parents, and even the community were involved in some way with the technology plan. The core essentials of the district include a section on aligned resources, which focuses resources on instructional improvement in order to meet its students' needs. Shared leadership is another factor in the successful planning and use of the district technology plan because it provides a collaborative culture in which to sustain instructional improvement. School laptops, non-English language resources, Internet resources in Spanish, and bilingual/total immersion programs all add to the district's plan. Essentially, this gives students who might be disenfranchised access to technology. In addition, many schools in the district provide special laptop access or the ability to take home computers for student use.

Funding the Technology Plan

In an era of general economic recession and school budget cuts, school administrators must focus on the challenge of securing funding for the digital age technology resources that will support the strategic plan (NETS.A Standard 1.c). Governmental funding is also available in most states to support educational change with technology. Some districts are using the new E-Rate discounts to obtain needed funding for wireless access devices to the Internet. However, participation in these programs requires that districts have technology plans in place: "To emphasize further the importance of planning, the U.S. federal government now requires school districts to have approved technology plans to participate in the Universal Service Fund program, commonly known as the E-Rate program" (Picciano, 2011, p. 10). Most states require districts to have technology plans in place before applying for technology grants under the No Child Left Behind legislation.

In addition to applying for funding for new technology, school leaders should also be advocates for the availability of such fiscal resources on local, state, and national levels. On the local level, principals and superintendents must work with budget committees, school boards, and the general community to support technology-infused educational practices (Marzano and Waters, 2009). NETP Goal 4 has a focus on interoperability capacity that is relevant to district-level leadership and is discussed in more detail in Chapter 4.

District-level data should not only be concerned with administrative management (Waters, 2011) but also with integrating data and networks for curriculum frameworks, special education information, teacher evaluation and professional development reporting (Ormiston, 2011), adequate yearly progress reporting under the No Child Left Behind Act, contract negotiation data, and budgeting. On the state and national levels, school administrators should be actively involved in professional organizations that promote effective educational practices in the digital age. State laws on curriculum standards and testing are some examples of areas in which school leaders should have input. Nationally, there is legislation on Race to the Top, broadband connectivity (Picciano, 2011), students with disabilities, and the No Child Left Behind Act that is vital to the decisions made by school leaders across the country.

TIPS FOR SCHOOL LEADERS

1 Use expert advice from the state department of education to assist in setting criteria for the technology plan before writing it.

2 Have multiple stakeholders' input in writing the technology plan, such as representatives from the district, building, and community levels.

3 Consider that technical and funding aspects are as important as curriculum, so include the technology coordinator and the business manager in the technology planning.

4 Do a needs assessment before writing the technology plan to ascertain what the district does and does not have in place.

5 Link the technology plan to the district mission statement in order to more fully meet the needs of all students. Refer to the Pomona Unified School District Technology Mission Statement and observe how it is the driving force for this district's technology use plan.

6 Rethink traditional assumptions about schooling in planning for technology use and in ensuring student progress to graduation; and learn about the newer competency-based instruction models.

7 Investigate the E-Rate discounts in order to obtain funding for wireless access devices to the Internet in your school district.

Summary

In this first chapter of six in *Educational Leadership and Technology: Preparing School Administrators for a Digital Age*, readers are introduced to the National Education Technology Plan goal of improving productivity and student achievement in America's schools and the International Society of Education's standard of planning educational technology with visionary leadership. A review of effective schools research indicates the need to involve multiple stakeholders in a well-funded technology plan. A technology plan from the Pomona Unified School District is a model that could be adapted by school leaders to their own districts. Additional applications from research to practice indicate how leaders should link virtual schooling to competency-based instruction. In the next chapter, the key role of educational administrators in using digital age tools to lead teachers in engaging and assessing learners is explored.

School administrators who rate themselves and their schools or districts with scores of 5 and 4 are already meeting the standards indicated in those items. Ratings of 1 or 2 would indicate areas of needed professional growth by either the school district, or the school leader, or both in order to meet the NETS.A standards or NETP goals.

TABLE 1.1 School Administrator's Technology Leadership Self-Assessment Survey: Technology Planning (Chapter 1)

Directions: Please respond to each item by circling a number from 1 to 5, where 5 = strongly agree; 4 = agree; 3 = neutral; 2 = disagree; 1 = strongly disagree.

This survey is based on National Education Technology Plan (NETP) Goal 5 (NETP 5.1 to 5.4) and National Educational Technology Standards and Performance Indicators for Administrators (NETS.A) Standard 1 (NETS.A 1.a, 1.b, 1.c).

5 = strongly agree (SA); 4 = agree (A); 3 = neutral (N); 2 = disagree (D); 1 = strongly disagree (SD)	SA	A	N	D	SD
1 Our district has effective measures of student outcomes (NETP 5.1).	5	4	3	2	1
2 Our district uses latest technologies to manage costs, including purchasing and bidding (NETP 5.1).	5	4	3	2	1
3 I am a proponent of competency-based learning and achievement (NETP 5.2).	5	4	3	2	1
4 I believe that our students are dropping out because they are disengaged from school (NETP 5.2).	5	4	3	2	1
5 I believe that virtual or online or blended learning is effective for potential dropouts (NETP 5.2).	5	4	3	2	1
6 I believe in multi-aged groupings (NETP 5.2).	5	4	3	2	1
7 I believe in flexibly scheduled classes on the secondary level (NETP 5.2).	5	4	3	2	1
8 I believe in extended learning time, such as adding instructional time to the school year (NETP 5.2).	5	4	3	2	1
9 Data in my school or district is collected on how technology supports instruction (NETP 5.3).	5	4	3	2	1
10 Technology effectively tracks student P-12 progress in my district (NETP 5.4).	5	4	3	2	1
11 Technology is used for interventions to lower the dropout rate in our schools (NETP 5.4).	5	4	3	2	1
12 Technology is effectively used to prepare our students for careers and/or college (NETP 5.4).	5	4	3	2	1

5 = strongly agree (SA); 4 = agree (A); 3 = neutral (N); 2 = disagree (D); 1 = strongly disagree (SD)	SA	A	N	D	SD
13 I agree that the "dropout age" should be 18 (NETP 5.4).	5	4	3	2	1
14 Electronic portfolios of student work are mandated in my school and district (NETP 5.4).	5	4	3	2	1
15 Our school and district technology plan uses digital age resources to (NETS.A 1.a):					
(a) meet and exceed learning goals;	5	4	3	2	1
(b) support effective instructional practice;	5	4	3	2	1
(c) maximize performance of school and district administrators.	5	4	3	2	1
16 Our technology planning is ongoing and uses the latest in digital technologies (NETS.A 1.b)	5	4	3	2	1
17 I advocate for policies and funding to support a technology-infused plan on the (NETS.A 1.c):					
(a) building level;	5	4	3	2	1
(b) district level;	5	4	3	2	1
(c) state level;	5	4	3	2	1
(d) national level.	5	4	3	2	1

V. E. Garland and C. Tadeja, 2012

DISCUSSION QUESTIONS

1 What would you consider are some of the most important aspects of implementing technology standards in your organization?

2 Thinking globally, what are some of the emerging technologies which your school district should adopt? How might you utilize these to meet the needs of the professional educator to help prepare student learners?

3 Describe the kind of technology plan that you have now in your organization. How did you promote collaboration among all stakeholders in writing your plan?

4 The leader's self-reflection for this chapter indicates that there are many challenges in implementing an effective three-year technology plan. Discuss the similar or different challenges which you or your district might face as a technology plan is being developed.

5 Based on your responses to the self-assessment for Chapter 1, what are the next steps you might take in technology planning for your school or district? What technology resources would you need in your own professional e-portfolio in order to assist you in achieving your goals?

2
Leading Instruction with New Technologies

Synopsis

How are you leading the use of digital age technologies in instruction? Do teachers in your school use the same social networking tools in the classroom that students are using in their daily lives outside of school? The second chapter addresses NETP Goals 1 and 2 on instruction and assessment and the ISTE NETS.A Standard 2 of implementing a "digital-age learning culture." School administrators on all levels need to be true instructional leaders in order to assist teachers in meeting the 21st-century needs of students in classrooms and in online learning environments. This chapter also focuses on embedding technology in assessment practices. It blends theory and practice, offering cost-effective, practical advice for the effective implementation of current technologies in the instruction and evaluation of pre-K-12 learners, both nationally and globally. In addition, the authors explore the latest in digital age tools, such as augmented reality technologies and neuro-headsets for greater student engagement in learning.

In the following leader reflections, senior directors of technology services in two school districts, one on the West Coast and the other on the East Coast, comment on this new digital learning culture and its implications for changes in curriculum, instruction, and assessment strategies.

Reflections of a Director of Integrated Technology in San Diego, California

Students today participate in a digital learning culture that encompasses their lives 24/7. Yet, currently, this digital learning culture exists predominately outside the school day. In a digital learning culture, literacy is more than text; it includes sound and screen as well. Recognizing that the nature of literacy itself is changing requires the critical understanding that technology enables students and teachers to take learning anywhere, anytime, through mobile technology devices. One of the most powerful innovative instructional experiences I've had was leading and managing a one-to-one mobile learning initiative.

There is little doubt that mobile learning devices transform how and when students learn. My own experience in leading such an initiative clearly illustrates the transformative nature of empowering students with individual devices. Equipping students with mobile technology definitely changes the playing field for everyone involved: students, teachers, parents, and administrators. Administrators in a one-to-one learning initiative witness first-hand the change these devices bring to the learning environment through a reinvention of curriculum, teaching, and assessment opportunities. These devices not only support but also demand a learning environment social in nature. The students use the technology to learn, meet, play, and socialize in interconnected ways that afford them real opportunities to make learning replicate real life; these social network tools can quickly become part of their learning experience and are rarely far from the student's reach. In essence, mobile technologies engage students in personalized learning and become extensions of their memory, creativity, and imagination – they become tools to "think with" and offer opportunities to interact with the world in authentic ways.

Understanding how today's children learn, think, work, and live in a digital world is critical if a digital learning culture is to become a part of the fabric of school life. You cannot have a digital learning culture when access is limited to specific times and places. Students with access to technology for only part of the school day cannot truly participate in a digital learning culture. I have found that individual mobile technologies are the key ingredient for promoting and creating a digital learning culture. Individual devices provide the catalyst for transforming a school learning culture from a static didactic experience into an interactive, mutually constructed learning experience. Teachers can no longer ignore the computer labs in the school or the small cluster of desktop units at the back of the room. Every student has a mobile device at his or her desk to use in ways that support individual learning styles and needs.

As part of several digital learning initiatives, I witnessed transformative shifts in student and teacher interactions. Students began suggesting new ways teachers could utilize the technology to be more efficient, more creative, or more informative. Their roles quickly became more collaborative and supportive. This shift and change in the student/teacher relationship is one of the most critical changes necessary to support a digital learning culture. Teachers quickly discovered and embraced the idea that now all learners (students, teachers, and administrators) are nomadic. Now conversations can occur across time and space, extending beyond the traditional block schedule and school day. It is this shift in interaction, in relationship, and in time and space that creates a true digital learning culture.

Students need and want uninterrupted access to rich curriculum, mobile devices, social learning interactions, and immediate feedback in order to learn, achieve, and grow. Innovative instructional leaders leverage technology for educational goals, creating assessment-centered learning environments that provide immediate information on what students are learning. There is no better way to address the needs of diverse learners than through such environments. When students don't learn, the community suffers. To meet the needs of diverse learners, assessments need to be ongoing and prescriptive so that every student is a valued member of society. Technology, in general, and more specifically mobile technology, contributes to formative, ongoing, and prescriptive assessment through online test-taking, online learning surveys powered by student response systems, online discussion and debate activities, intelligent remediation software, technology-powered writing quality assessment, project-based learning opportunities, digital portfolios, and so much more. To meet the needs of diverse learners we must utilize and develop assessment tools for use throughout the year to monitor individual and group learning.

My experience has shown that when the assessment data and analytical tools are provided to both teachers and students "just in time," learning grows, achievement improves, and diverse learners are empowered to be responsible for both self-assessment and their own learning.

Karen Connaghan is the senior director of integrated technology services for the entire San Diego County Office of Education in San Diego, California.

Reflections of an Instructional Technology Leader in Georgia

For a number of years the trend has been to place considerable (if not too much weight) on the value of standardized tests in monitoring student achievement. It's certainly understandable given focus on making AYP [adequate yearly progress]. However, it is certainly not the best assessment "diet" for students or life-long learning.

In Forsyth, we use a balanced assessment program consisting of a combination of standardized tests and classroom assessments. Both types of assessments are used for developing an accurate picture of a student's overall academic achievement. Standardized tests administered in Forsyth County include a combination of norm-referenced tests, criterion-referenced tests, and ability and achievement tests. Classroom assessments are correlated to the Georgia Performance Standards and provide teachers [with] an ongoing measurement of student progress. Classroom assessments may include, but are not limited to, student portfolios, performance assessments, observations, benchmark tests and writing samples.

One way of considering how to balance the scales of assessment is by considering the question: If you were putting the one-time-a-year standardized test on one side of a scale and classroom assessments on the other, which side should weigh more? This question is valuable in prompting discussion about types of assessment. It may also be helpful to draw models, which represent the various forms of assessment and the weight they hold in the overall Balanced Assessment Diet.

Consider also the move towards the Common Core Standards. These standards and the assessments being developed to go along with them are *performance based*. To quote my colleague, Dr. Lissa Pijanowski, Forsyth County Schools associate superintendent for academics and accountability: "The classroom implications for this next generation of assessments is that a significant emphasis must be placed on providing students with integrated performance tasks that call on creative problem-solving skills and higher-order thinking. Students will be required to apply their knowledge and demonstrate a deeper understanding of content."

Jill Hobson is the director of instructional technology for Forsyth County Schools, Georgia. Working with media specialists and instructional technology specialists, Jill focuses on achieving the vision of using classroom technology to engage students in asking questions and choosing tools to facilitate real world problem-solving. Jill was named one of Technology and Learning's Top 100 most important people in educational technology. She has been on the National School Board Association's "Twenty to Watch," a list of 20 emerging leaders in technology.

Introduction

By now the digital age learning culture should have driven the last nail in the coffin of teacher-centered instruction. Effective educational uses of the social networking tools popular with the iGeneration engage today's learners far more than the lectures of the past. This chapter deals with the most crucial aspect of school administration today, that of leading instructional innovations in order to improve student achievement through greater learner engagement. In this chapter, the authors explain how educational administrators can implement NETP Goals 1 and 2 of embedding new technologies in learning, assessment, and teaching within the digital age learning culture described in NETS.A Standard 2. This chapter emphasizes the key role of the school administrator in leading the use of new educational technologies for all students, especially those in underserved school communities. In order for the building-level leader to attain the goal of high levels of student productivity in his or her school, there must be strategies in place for meaningful and technology-powered assessments for preparing students to compete globally.

Digital Age Learning Culture

iGeneration

The first widespread users of the Internet are commonly known as Generation Y and they can be defined as people born during the 1980s and early 1990s (McCoog, 2008). The youngest of this cohort are now occupying seats in America's high schools. Then there is the latest generational tag (Gen Z) that has been assigned to those born from the late 1990s to the present. Digital technology to them is almost a birth right, and schools must accommodate that. This generation is also often referred to as the Millennials (as is Gen Y), a reference not only to their birth dates, but also to their connection to technology (Howe and Strauss, 2000). In addition, the more generalized iGeneration term comes from the identification of individuals who have grown up with technology. They use the Internet known as Web 2.0, which is more dynamic and collaborative than its predecessor.

The iGeneration has embraced the emerging wireless technologies that give them opportunities unavailable to any previous generation (Rosen, 2011). Those who have grown up using the new social networking tools, or the iGeneration users, have a new set of Web 2.0 tools which teachers need to use in order to help students. These technologies are both interactive and immersive. The results of a recent study found that today's 8- to 18-year-olds spend almost eight hours each day on entertainment media (Kaiser Family Foundation, 2009). Educators are now uniquely positioned to enhance instruction with some of the same wireless media devices that students are using so pervasively in their social milieu.

The use of mobile learning devices is becoming more and more prominent in society as it also paves the way for learning at the school site level. Participatory devices, which were popular with the introduction of immediate response systems such as "clickers," are now moving on to the mobile realm. Applications and software are being developed at a fast rate to accommodate the needs of both teachers and the general public. For instance, participatory devices have also opened the way for collaborative data learning where students can engage with one another in a group investigation. This is important because many of the lifelong skills we learn and use in adulthood while working in teams can be garnered from these types of collaborative activities (Roschelle, 2003).

Schools are often charged with the challenge of ensuring personalized learning. The computer is a perfect tool to accomplish this goal of individualized instruction. Not only does each student have his or her own device but the device itself can be programmed to work and learn according to that student's best learning modality and intelligence. For example, if a child is a musical learner, then that computer can be programmed so that each lesson is done with as much musical modality as possible. Each lesson, unit, activity, and even assessment can accommodate the unique needs of each student. Traditional forms of teacher-centered instruction do not differentiate between students because it is a classroom setting in which a single teacher tries to address all students in his or her class. Administrators need to know the potential of the computer applications for differentiating learning, including supporting teachers' use of varied delivery modules to meet each student's best learning modality.

How is the iGeneration communicating? Are teachers in your schools using those same communication technologies for instructional purposes? Educational leaders should support those digital age networking tools in instructional practices that will be effective in developing students' 21st-century skills. There are numerous wireless and social media tools that are now prevalent. In order for students to reach high levels of engagement and achievement, school administrators should have in and out of school Internet access for teachers and students through wireless devices with multimedia capacities. These mobile platforms can be instructional tools to enhance students' creativity, ethical citizenship, and academic achievement.

A few years ago, many colleges provided their students, specifically their incoming freshmen class, with new and "free" laptops or other electronic devices. This was done, in part, to entice students to come to their school. Perhaps another and better reason for this was to address the issue of the electronic age and the media-rich learning that is possible with the use of a personal device. It is no surprise that this enticement of using digital age tools in learning would be very popular among students. Today, there is a veritable revolution taking place with the advent of media-rich social networking devices such as MP3 players, iPads, smartphones, tablet PCs, and other devices.

Today's classroom learners are no longer interested in the old lecture format and they are tuning out the teachers who simply stand and deliver their lectures (Schrum and Levin, 2009). So what is a teacher to do to motivate his or her students to learn? Perhaps equally important is to ask what can administrators do to help promote a digital age learning culture? As Prensky (2008, p. 43) describes: "School instruction is still mostly cookie cutter and one size fits all, despite the fact that we live in an era of customization – students continually customize their buddy lists, photos, ring tones, cell phone skins, websites, blogs, and Facebook pages."

It is important that the customization of technology in a digital age is also adapted to our learners' needs. These students must be taught in the way they learn by using the 21st-century skills they already possess (Tadeja, 2010). Twenty-first century teaching involves a balance of the objectives of the teacher with the needs and input of the students. For this reason, learning objectives should be specific but flexible by allowing customization. Today's students are acquiring 21st-century skills outside the classrooms and this surprises teachers. Twenty-first century learners and young teachers have taught themselves to network and find solutions. Because of this, they expect to have the same experiences in learning and teaching. This trend has rightfully caused a stir in the education community and has called for reform in how and what to teach (McCoog, 2008). Students must be considered at the planning, delivery, and assessment stages of instruction. Teachers should not be afraid to ask their students their opinions. They should consider what they could contribute during the planning of a lesson (Tadeja, 2010). Administrators need to have the same technology skills as their teachers and students in order to support them, provide them with challenges, and then guide them on their way to solutions.

Some of the latest networking tools provide opportunities for school leaders, teachers, and students to make connections. The use of the cell phone is one such tool. Poll Everywhere is a free real-time polling feature that allows users to cast their votes with their cell phones. For instance, a teacher may survey the class on a pop quiz or a principal might get the teachers' views on certain issues. Although some schools limit the use of cell phones, digital age technologies are becoming mobile and more students and adults are using their cell phones to conduct everything from banking to schooling to purchasing e-books, stamps, and vending machine products.

However, not all teachers, administrators, and learners have access to the new social networking tools. It is especially important for superintendents, principals, and technology coordinators to find ways to close the "digital divide" between students in their districts. Large organizations such as Dell and Verizon have recently provided grants and gifts of technology to many underserved children across the country (Schwartz, 2010). This effort addresses the National Education Technology Plan's similar concern with diversity issues regarding underserved students needing technology. All students should experience for themselves the multimedia aspects of communicating and sharing ideas with others. Although technology alone does not provide good pedagogy (Twigg, 2005), digital age tools can jump-start the creativity of each child. In the "Tips for School Leaders" at the end of this chapter, further Golden Rules for Teaching with Technology are presented.

ISTE NETS.A Standard 2

In the previous section, you read how iGeneration students already have social networking technology tools that enable them to connect with almost anyone, anywhere, anytime. The importance of meeting the learning needs of the iGeneration is outlined in ISTE NETS.A Standard 2, the "Digital-Age Learning Culture":

> Educational Administrators create, promote, and sustain a dynamic, digital-age learning culture that provides a rigorous, relevant, and engaging education for all students. Educational Administrators:
>
> (a) ensure instructional innovation focused on continuous improvement of digital-age learning;
>
> (b) model and promote the frequent and effective use of technology for learning;
>
> (c) provide learner-centered environments equipped with technology and learning resources to meet the individual, diverse needs of all learners;
>
> (d) ensure effective practice in the study of technology and its infusion across the curriculum;
>
> (e) promote and participate in local, national, and global learning communities that stimulate innovation, creativity, and digital-age collaboration.
>
> (ISTE, 2009, p. 11)

This second NETS.A standard emphasizes the need to provide opportunities for educators to fully implement the 21st-century technology tools described in the iGeneration section (NETS.A Standard 2). School leaders can accomplish this, in part, by allowing teachers to become instructional innovators. Learning in the digital age is a student-centered, collaborative process. For example, when one of this book's authors first began teaching, he told others that students learn best when there is an "MTV style of learning" presented in class. At that time, he explored the different ways in which students learn with "jazzed up PowerPoints" for course content or presenting the day's agenda on flat-screen television. Even though this California teacher wanted to explore new technologies, there were no supervisors to assist in embedding digital tools in his lessons. However, most school districts now have technology coordinators and more "tech savvy" administrators, who should be available to give expertise and support for teachers who wish to take risks with emerging technologies.

School principals, technology coordinators, and program coordinators should therefore encourage instructional innovations which are based on advances in digital age learning (Hokanson et al., 2008). The role of today's principal is vastly different from the role of yesterday's. The inclusion of technology has improved our communication and has changed the way in which principals collaborate with others. The principal is no longer the only educator with all the answers to the problems at his or her school. It is imperative that the principal acts as a collaborator and facilitator with learning teams at his or her site. This is done in order to advance professional practice and increase student achievement (Roberson et al., 2009).

Instructional innovation includes having to find some of the latest technologies to use at each site. Tech entrepreneur Nam Do is a regular guest speaker at Harvard Business School and Stanford University. He recently developed a headset that basically reads your mind! In this next-generation human–computer interface, he showcases how simply thinking about it by use of a small headset can move virtual objects. The applications are far reaching and can transcend classroom learning in ways never before imagined (Takahashi, 2007). The current system runs on most Windows-based computers and costs less than many of today's popular software programs.

Not all learners have a need for such a neuro-headset; but instructional innovation – whether in the classroom or in the boardroom – means that leaders are brought up to date on the latest technology that can transform artistic and creative expression and create gaming worlds. Educational leaders do not have to know exactly how such devices work. But they do have to have the tenacity to envision how their use could compel educators to engage learners more effectively.

Furthermore, the school principal, program director, or superintendent must also take risks in using emerging technologies in his or her own practice (NETS.A Standard 2). Since technology has a direct impact upon learning, it is necessary for leaders to act as facilitators and change agents in the effective instructional uses of technology. Teachers often observe or consult with other teachers who find success in the classroom, especially when using technology. These teachers want to know what works, why it works, and, more importantly, how this same strategy can be used in their own classrooms. When a teacher has found a way to utilize a lesson or strategy in technology, it will be important for the school leader to capture that strategy and allow other teachers the chance to see if it will work for them. School administrators, particularly principals, should plan staff development days for teachers to collaboratively discover new technologies as one way of promoting the effective use of technology. Professional development opportunities are explored in more depth in the following chapter.

Social Networking Tools

You have read how fostering innovative practices provides students with greater opportunities for success. School leaders and teacher trainers must therefore leverage social networking technology tools in order to enhance professional practice. Although many students and young teachers of the "digital native" generation use laptops, smart phones, and handheld gaming devices, they do not necessarily know how to use these wireless devices in learning and instruction. Unfortunately, many veteran teachers and administrators are "digital immigrants," perhaps unfamiliar with many of the recent advances in social networking tools and their applications to educational practice.

The way in which "digital natives" communicate is different from the way in which "digital immigrants" communicate. Conversely, a "digital native" will learn differently than their mostly older "digital immigrant" counterparts. The integration of social media within the lives of the "digital native" is said to have isolated them as social hermits. However, this may not be the case in education because many "net generation" students and young teachers and administrators form online communities through discussion boards, blogs, or other online networks. "Digital natives" do expect their teachers and administrators to use technology in ways that will suit their digital age learning styles.

Social networking platforms are ideal for creating local and even global groups of professional educators, working collaboratively to share best practices and resources to meet students' diverse learning needs. Online communities allow educators to be life-long career professionals by enabling them to take online courses or workshops, access experts in their fields, obtain timely resources and research studies, and collaborate with their colleagues in designing digital age learning activities. Chapter 3 further explores the availability of networked learning communities for meeting the professional development needs of educators.

Engaging and Empowering Learners

The previous section is focused on how NETS.A Standard 2 addresses the digital age learning culture of the iGeneration. The first goal of the National Education Technology Plan (NETP Goal 1) gives us more inspiration on providing American students 24/7 access to digital age learning experiences that will enable them to be active and innovative participants in the global arena. It is similar to the ISTE National Educational Technology Standards for Students (NETS.S) that should be implemented by school administrators who coordinate curriculum standards and supervise instruction. The six key NETS.S competencies for students are to use digital age tools in creativity and innovation; communication and collaboration; research and information fluency; critical thinking; digital citizenship; and technology operations. School leaders, particularly superintendents, principals, and program directors, should ensure that these technology skill sets are fully addressed in their schools or districts. When learners fully meet both the NETS.S standards and the first NETP goal, then they can become life-long learners, with opportunities to further engage in online communities. Here are the components of NETP Goal 1: "Learning: Engage and Empower":

1.0 Learning: All learners will have engaging and empowering learning experiences both in and out of school that prepare them to be active, creative, knowledgeable, and ethical participants in our globally networked society.

1.1 States should continue to revise, create, and implement standards and learning objectives using technology for all content areas that reflect 21st century expertise and the power of technology to improve learning.

1.2 States, districts, and others should develop and implement learning resources that use technology to embody design principles from the learning sciences.

1.3 States, districts, and others should develop and implement learning resources that exploit the flexibility and power of technology to reach all learners anytime and anywhere.

1.4 Use advances in learning sciences and technology to enhance STEM learning and develop, adopt, and evaluate new methodologies with the potential to inspire and enable all learners to excel in STEM.

(U.S. Department of Education, 2010, pp. 23–24)

The shortage of learning opportunities in some areas and in certain disciplines is an issue that can be immediately addressed with inexpensive digital age tools. Technology can be harnessed to meet the needs of underserved students living in rural areas or for those without access to science, technology, engineering, and mathematics (STEM) subjects through online and hybrid (online and in-class) course offerings. Virtual courses or "cyber-courses" are important because there are significant shortages of teachers in STEM and rural areas. For instance, only one third of all physics teachers have actually had a course in physics or physics education, and many of the "least able" teachers are in rural schools (U.S. Department of Education, 2010). Online courses of quality are those that use the most effective teaching methods in diverse courses, particularly those in STEM subject areas, easily available to all students, regardless of geographical location.

There is a need for both pre-service and in-service teachers and school administrators to improve their digital literacy skills so that these professional educators can embed technological advances in assignments for learners. In addition to the ASSISTment, River City, and Math Forum interactive online programs available to STEM teachers, some websites give actual lessons that have proven success. The U.K.-based SchoolsWorld TV (http://www.schoolsworld.tv), for instance, has beginning lessons in English, mathematics, and science. They have 116 videos in the math series for secondary-level teachers with content ranging from engineering to cosmetology. One such motivating lesson is "Hidden Patterns in Durham Cathedral," in which the mathematician Steve Humble uses the architectural details of the cathedral to explore mathematical applications in the real world.

21st-Century Digital Skills

The Partnership for 21st-Century Skills organization states in its mission statement that its aim is to build collaborative partnerships among education, business, community, and government leaders. In many ways, its mission is to equip teachers with the tools that students will need to learn in the 21st century. It has dedicated its cause to helping students gain the necessary skills to adapt, learn, and thrive in the world of technology today. The Partnership for 21st Century Skills group has a framework based on essential skills that students need in order to better prepare them to work and succeed in this century. As leaders, it is important to look at these skills and equip teachers with as much support as possible in order for them to succeed in this endeavor. The guidelines of this partnership are based primarily on the National Educational Technology Standards, one of the two professional frameworks according to which this book is organized. More detail is given to forming partnerships such as this one in Chapter 5.

Another one of the more revolutionary ways to help students prepare for the demanding needs of the 21st century is to teach them how to collaborate and create content online. Schrum and Levin (2009) advocate the creation of student portfolios, in which multimedia content has been created with such Web 2.0 tools as Google Pages and Google Docs Presentation. Other presentation tools, such as Prezi and SlideShare, provide opportunities to design presentation pieces using non-linear methods. Despite the numerous PowerPoint presentations designed each day by various users around the globe, presentation software is now being used and designed with the sequencing that was once constraining to some individuals. Video presentation tools such as Animoto, XtraNormal, and GoAnimate now make it easy for students to create high-quality videos using sophisticated designs and expensive-looking interfaces.

However, the current challenge for using "technology without boundaries" is to design new learning environments that easily support the established pedagogical goals of the school district. One way in which this can be done is for teachers to design courses that drive student engagement. Another way to support curriculum goals is for school leaders to encourage learner participation in user-generated content. Nothing is more powerful in student engagement than when a class member authors content and has to either defend it or connect it with the course being taught. Some students in the Coalition of Essential Schools, such as Noble High School in Chapter 3's leader reflection piece, submit their own work in portfolios and defend the e-portfolio content as a culminating senior-year activity. Despite what we might not like about how students communicate today, they are using their own content in blogs, wikis, and other forums to discuss their thoughts, feelings, and ideas. We must harness this desire and let it be a part of the course design.

Smartphones are already used by this generation of students as the new wave of learning. If course designers or educational leaders do not optimize content as mobile ready, then they could be behind the times. One way to directly connect the online and offline worlds is through the use of Quick Response (QR) codes. These codes, which essentially allow users to capture information and then retrieve it later, are now being used in various school districts across the country. A free QR code generator called Kaywa allows users to generate their own codes and reference them to a website or other pertinent and powerful content. A science teacher, therefore, can generate a code and replicate it on a handout so that students can go home and activate the code on their Internet access devices, revealing additional information on the content or subject presented. The goal is to increase engagement and interactivity with the content. Students can no longer afford to sit and listen to the expert in the classroom: they need more engagement.

Adaptive Learning

The leaders' support of adaptive technologies in instruction is key to integrating some of the latest technologies to help students learn. Adaptive learning is an exciting interdisciplinary concept. In the second section of this primary goal (NETP Goal 1.2), there is a call for instructional experts from the fields of education, social science, neuroscience, and cognitive theory to collaborate in the design of technology-embedded academic skills. Adaptive learning is an educational method which uses computers as interactive teaching devices. The term has its origins in artificial intelligence theory, in which systems can re-program themselves according to changes in environmental factors. In education, adaptive learning refers to the use of computerized methods of presenting content to meet the individual needs of learners. In other words, the digitized material adapts to the student's mastery levels and learning styles. With adaptive learning, teachers use technological advances in order to facilitate learning on three progressive and sequential levels: factual, procedural, and motivational. For instance, if a student has difficulty grasping concepts, a teacher might initiate changes in the technology-enhanced module in order for the student to understand the facts behind that particular concept. If that particular intervention is not successful, then a different change in methods and perhaps a motivational technique might be introduced with adaptive learning technologies.

Administrators can thus support the primary objective of adaptive learning so that students can apply content knowledge to new situations. Some powerful examples of adaptive learning are through augmented reality platforms and games. Augmented reality combines both virtual and real-world elements, which interact simultaneously. Members of a robotics club could, for instance, point a camera onto a piece of paper, and the complexities of the club's robot design would appear on both the original paper document and an attached computer screen. The computer user could then manipulate the robot to look around it, above it, and within it, all without touching or destroying the delicate object. There are also phone applications that allow a user to point a camera down a busy intersection, and the phone will automatically embed or superimpose points of interest along that intersection in order for the user to determine where to go to a museum, bookstore, electronics shop, or to locate environmental sites, all by simply looking at the augmented reality screen of his or her phone. This phenomenon is sometimes referred to as geo-tagging or geo-locating, but the concept is having the student understand the elements around him or her and to make informed decisions. For instance, Global Positioning Systems (GPS) on classroom-supplied wireless handhelds can access local learning resources as they engage and motivate young learners (Johnson et al., 2010).

Applications like these are now being used in the medical and commercial fields; but the possibilities in education are astounding and limitless. Special education has already taken an interest in the use of augmented reality software to help these learners better understand lessons or to utilize manipulatives that were once considered technologically impossible. Websites and professional education conferences now highlight the use of augmented reality in studying the solar system, in learning language, or in repairing automotives.

In one augmented reality studio that the authors visited, students wore dark but translucent goggles and watched both real-world and computer-generated images embedded together. Students could then watch and interact with the solar systems in ways never imagined before. Students could look around Venus or study the rings around Saturn in depth from the comforts of the classroom. They could have a full 360-degree view of a complex DNA molecule. Students could then write about their experiences or provide formative feedback to each other in order to get a sense of their experience or measure what they had learned. In simple studios that one can build in the classroom or even at home, students place a simple sheet of paper in front of them and point it to a nearby webcam. After an initial code is captured onto the computer, the paper soon reflects a three-dimensional object that students can then study. If the student moves the three-dimensional object, which is essentially the piece of paper, then that object moves. Students can then lift the object up, look underneath it, and point their fingers through the object, and the computer on screen will mimic the movement but replace it with the white sheet of paper that the student is holding. Students were fascinated with this concept since they can now look at a three-dimensional camshaft on a car or a heart valve and study the intricate features within all without having to remove the whole engine or the heart itself. This can all be done within the confines of a student's home or at the school and without the use of expensive equipment. With augmented reality, students can develop real-life skills in modeling objects. Students can, for example, perform diagnostics on a vehicle without the hassle or inconvenience of getting underneath the hood of a car. Students in an interior design class can look at a model of a home or room and consider different design schemes without having to actually paint the room or rearrange furnishings.

As an administrator, you can support the use of emerging technologies in instruction, including the adaptive learning tools described in this section, without compromising the district-mandated curriculum goals. We have provided you with examples of constructivist applications of digital tools, such as augmented reality platforms, in order to motivate student learning. Administrators and technology coordinators should try to purchase and provide teacher training in some of these very engaging digital age tools. The professional development opportunities available for educators are further described in the next chapter.

Universal Design for Learning (UDL)

The potential of online learning is limitless! Digital age technology advances allow students to learn anytime (NETP Goal 1.3) in school districts, homes, and just about anywhere across the globe. This 24/7 instruction can be online, with open courseware, and based on the Universal Design for Learning (UDL) concept of making learning opportunities available to all students. According to the National Center on Universal Design for Learning, the UDL framework helps educators to develop curricula in specific ways in order to meet the needs of all learners. The three major tenets of UDL focus on "representation, expression, and engagement" by students in the learning process (http://www.udlcenter.org/aboutudl/udlguidelines). The three main principles of UDL coincide with emerging technologies in the following ways:

1. Multiple instructional strategies to meet the needs of diverse learning styles can include interactive online media or e-books (representation).

2. Flexible student demonstration of competency mastery would be facilitated with concept mapping software (expression).
3. Varied approaches to engage and motivate students to learn would certainly benefit from online collaborations with multimedia platforms (engagement).

Science, Technology, Engineering, and Mathematics (STEM)

Why are American students performing poorly on the science and mathematics sections of international tests in comparison with students in other developed nations? The last segment of the first NETP goal (1.4) is focused on preparing American students for science, technology, engineering, and mathematics (STEM) professions. Although technological advances have transformed these scientific and mathematical fields, many schools are still using outdated methods to teach these subjects. In the digital age, students need to be able to more effectively communicate and manipulate data and knowledge in STEM content areas in order to be complex problem-solvers.

STEM has received much attention because of the United States' loss of world status in science and engineering (National Science Board, 2010) in comparison to increasing achievements in these fields by some Asian countries, such as China, South Korea, Japan, and Malaysia. In response to the decline in the performance of U.S. students in STEM subjects on international tests (McKinsey and Company, 2009), in 2010 the national executive office provided "$250 million in private resources to attract, develop, reward and retain STEM educators" (U.S. Department of Education, 2010, p. 22). According to the Science, Technology, Engineering, and Mathematics (STEM) Education Coalition, there are other initiatives in STEM programs for teachers and students that can be found at the U.S. Department of Education or the National Science Foundation (http://www.stemedcoalition.org/). School superintendents and principals would be wise to tap into these resources in order to provide new opportunities for STEM learning in their schools and districts.

Digitally Excluded Learners

Think for a moment about the types of learners in your school district. Who might be digitally excluded? Some types of digital age instruction, such as UDL, are particularly important in serving the needs of marginalized learners: those students who are disabled, or from rural areas, or from low socio-economic areas, or from diverse cultures and languages. One of the goals of using technology tools is to decrease the achievement gap between the "haves" and the "have nots," otherwise known as the "digital divide." Some of the "have nots" are now becoming the "digitally excluded" because they cannot adequately access the Internet (Genachowski, 2011).

School administrators play a key role in ensuring that these four main groups of marginalized, "digitally excluded" learners (low-income and minority students; English language learners (ELLs); disabled students; and early childhood learners) get the 21st-century technology skills they need. Since students living in low socio-economic households are less likely to have technology supports at home, school leaders should implement one-laptop-per-student policies in which students can take computers home (refer to the leader reflection on the Maine laptop initiative in Chapter 3) or to libraries and schools which have extended hours for Internet access. As alternatives to presenting lessons in English, technology coordinators might make language translation software and multimedia applications available for ELLs in their districts. Principals and superintendents are legally bound to fulfill the Individualized Education Plans (IEPs) of special education students in their schools. Some of those supports might be the purchase of assistive technologies for disabled students, such as modified keyboards for learners with certain physical disabilities, text-to-speech readers for those with visual impairments, and signing avatars for students with hearing disabilities. Chapter 6 provides additional analysis of how to provide for underserved students.

Assessment

In order to reach the goal of increased student achievement, NETP authors recommend the use of current technologies and research in order to assess learning effectively (NETP Goal 2). In addition, a more standards-based assessment approach to student achievement aligns with the demand for accountability and transparency in educational practices by many educators, parents, and policy-makers. Superintendents and principals are also under considerable legal scrutiny with the accountability tenets of the No Child Left Behind Act provisions for state testing of students in all federally funded public schools.

The second NETP goal addresses the need to assess learning while it is occurring, rather than after the instruction has been completed. This is a mandate for schools and districts to use technology to improve not only student achievement but also instructional practices. Digital age assessments can give more timely feedback than traditional testing methods. These are the sections of NETP Goal 2: "Assessment: Measure What Matters":

> 2.0 Assessment: Our education system at all levels will leverage the power of technology to measure what matters and use assessment data for continuous improvement.

> 2.1 States, districts, and others should design, develop, and implement assessments that give students, educators, and other stakeholders' timely and actionable feedback about student learning to improve achievement and instructional practices.

> 2.2 Build the capacity of educators, educational institutions, and developers to use technology to improve assessment materials and processes for both formative and summative uses.

> 2.3 Conduct research and development that explores how embedded assessment technologies, such as simulations, collaboration environments, virtual worlds, games and cognitive tutors, can be used to engage and motivate learners while assessing complex skills.

> 2.4 Conduct research and development that explores how UDL can enable the best accommodations for all students to ensure we are assessing what we

intend to measure rather than extraneous abilities a student needs to respond to the assessment task.

2.5 Revise practices, policies, and regulations to ensure privacy and information protection while enabling a model of assessment that includes ongoing gathering and sharing of data for continuous improvement.

(U.S. Department of Education, 2010, pp. 37–38)

Formative and Summative Assessments

There is a clear emphasis on both formative and summative uses of new technology-based assessment tools in NETP Goal 2. The diagnosis of learning experiences for students during instruction is the formative approach in assessment, whereas the grading and accountability measurements of student achievement levels are the summative goals of evaluation systems. Formative assessments thus occur during instruction and allow for modifications, whereas summative evaluations occur upon the completion of instruction.

New assessment techniques with digital age tools increase both the quality and the quantity of formative and summative feedback to students. These technologies are far more effective than conventional testing methods, which are inadequate in measuring learning as it is occurring. For example, many schools are beginning to implement Quick Response devices, also known as classroom response systems, to increase student engagement during instruction. These devices give immediate and positive reinforcement and can result in greater collaboration among student peers. They were originally introduced by keynote speakers and some television game show hosts, who wanted to engage the audience members by having participants "click" their immediate responses to speeches or answers to questions. Response systems have since migrated into the educational world and now enable teachers to gauge learners' views on topics, as they are being taught. They have benefited students in being more engaged in their own learning experiences.

Teachers from all over the country have told the authors about certain ways in which they have used instant response systems. A high school math teacher in Connecticut once described how she used the system each time a new math concept was introduced. This was done to ensure that students could follow along with the new lesson as well as keep them engaged. Another teacher, of a Gainesville, Florida, sixth grade, told how she used it exclusively for vocabulary words. Whenever a new vocabulary word was introduced in a story or an exercise, the teacher would place the word on the instant response system to see if students knew the word, had ever seen the word, or had never seen or heard of it. The students' responses allowed the teacher to access their prior knowledge and better plan for the progression of the lesson as it occurred. Finally, a teacher from Altoona, Pennsylvania, made regular use of these systems with his high school students by giving learners a game device which added both visual and sound effects to better pique their interest. He later interviewed his students, who admitted that they did not think they were learning but had, in fact, learned the objective and the vocabulary being taught in subsequent assessments. In Singapore, another effective approach to student-centered learning is through the instructor's use of software called

Group Scribbles on whiteboards (Looi et al., 2010). With Group Scribbles, instructors can collaborate together in using common communication tools, such as sticky notes and markers. Teachers can use Group Scribbles and social networking tools, with which their students are most familiar, to give rapid in-class feedback, as well as to establish online communities of learners.

The use of digital portfolios is still increasing with the use of technology today. But housing digital portfolios has now gone to the clouds and most student work is both created and stored that way as well. It is a convenient method for students to house and access materials and products that they have created over their years in school. Some school districts are encouraging the use of digital portfolios as early as the third grade! Nevertheless, other school administrators are citing privacy issues and storage space. Universities such as those that are part of the Urban Universities Portfolio Project (UUPP) understand the value that digital portfolios provide, especially with the incoming students. The UUPP was designed and started with the help of six nationwide universities that developed institutional e-portfolio prototypes. The term e-portfolio is used in conjunction with digital portfolios. The result is a system of evaluations for digital portfolios. Administrators and technology coordinators can look through these to see what kinds of things colleges expect when determining the effectiveness of digital portfolios. Having students develop digital portfolios is ideal; but the complexities behind teaching how to develop one are challenging. Unfortunately, too many students do not spend enough time organizing the digital portfolio in a way that allows the viewer to easily follow its material. Unless provided with specific editing criteria, the student e-portfolios can become disorganized and overloaded with too much information. The Instructional Management System Global Learning Consortium provides numerous competencies to judge the organization and completeness of a digital portfolio (http://iport.iupui.edu/selfstudy/tl/milestones/uupp). Commercial sites such as TaskStream and Sakai have also built extensive components to house the use of digital portfolios.

Technology can also be used to connect key resources to student learning. At New Tech High in Napa Valley, California, aggregated assessments are linked to online grade books and e-learning portfolios. The "eCart" project in the Fairfax, Virginia, public school district is another example of a technology-based assessment system, which integrates online and in-house instructional resources into instructional improvement (U.S. Department of Education, 2010, pp. 34–35). These examples of best practices in schools across the globe indicate how school administrators might use similar emerging technologies to assess the ongoing learning of their student populations. The next steps could be to tie in what students learn in the classroom to what lifelong learning lessons they can take with them. Traditional learning can no longer sustain the individual learning needs of every learner. It is difficult for every teacher in every class period every day to address the numerous learning modalities of each student. Technology can assist the teacher in differentiating instruction through such methods as adaptive learning.

The federal government has recently subsidized the technology enhancement of school district assessment systems. The 2010 Race to the Top initiative of the U.S. Department of Education encouraged grant applications from those states that already had state-level tests to measure complex problem-solving. According to the director of the Race to the Top Competition, Joanne Weiss (2010), applicants for this federal funding were urged to take advantage of technology advances in assessments in order to provide effective performance tasks and applications, quick scoring and feedback to schools, as well as accommodation for diverse learners.

Assessment Management Systems (AMS) is one way to harness the power of assessment tools for a school district or university. Many AMS are commercially available for any enterprise and are managed by some of the most respected names in education, including Pearson and Edusoft. An AMS offers a wide variety of tools to help a school or school district manage their assessments. This could include collecting or analyzing data, or other services to include an e-portfolio collection service. Districts across the nation understand the value of data collection, and analyzing it quickly and accurately is a valuable commodity.

One model program for online formative assessment is the ASSISTment system in place in Worcester County Public Schools in Massachusetts. This web-based tutoring program, the result of a collaborative research effort between the Worcester Polytechnic Institute and the Carnegie Mellon University, teaches middle school mathematics concepts. It also gives teachers ongoing reports on students' progress towards mastering problem-solving mathematics activities (Feng et al., 2009). Interventions such as the ASSISTment program allow teachers to continually monitor and modify their instructional goals for both individuals and groups of students. School administrators should investigate the possibilities of partnerships such as these with local universities or colleges with teacher preparation programs.

When merged with effective assessment design, technology can improve the methods of evaluating student achievement. School administrators can harness the improvements in technology-enhanced testing on three levels: aggregating student assessment data, evaluating student learning when it is occurring, and involving key stakeholders in using assessments wisely (U.S. Department of Education, 2010). In order to support student learning on both formative and summative levels, test data needs to be taken and aggregated during and after instruction occurs so that teachers, schools, and districts can determine which individuals, subgroups, and entire schools are performing at expected levels. This information needs to be shared with teachers, parents, and students so that interventions can be properly implemented during instruction. An interconnected feedback system, developed with new technologies, can make data on student achievement available to school leaders and parents. This feedback system can be integrated by allowing all stakeholders access to the data. Administrators should find value in the use of the instant response and interconnected types of constant feedback to students. Teachers should give learners continuous opportunities to improve by providing them with meaningful feedback and the skills to achieve mastery. Unfortunately, students often receive scores back on an assessment, but with little or no feedback. Students would have difficulty with formative feedback unless it was interactive and allowed them to ask questions, as well as receive information not only from teachers, but also administrators and parents.

Looking at data assessment can be a daunting task. Ask any faculty member and he or she will tell you that making a connection between test scores and the learning that is taking place in classrooms is quite difficult. But it is also quite necessary. Online assessments should be conducted for diagnostic purposes in order to improve student learning. One way to do this is to disaggregate the scores by breaking up the data into small pieces and to focus in on certain areas. If teachers took an entire day to look at all of the data that comprised both their own individual students and that of the entire school, they would find this task intimidating and useless. No one educator can evaluate all student performance information and use it effectively. At the weekly staff meeting, for instance, staff can be introduced to one component or area in order to address this concern in the classroom.

The various models of teaching using technology encompass a wide range of tools. But many teachers have empowered the use of a "hook" to engage students in learning. Much like the use of an anticipatory set in the traditional lesson plan, a hook allows a teacher to capture the students' attention as they begin to engage in learning. A short video clip is one way to do this. Math classes often use Geometer Sketchpad while science classes use Probeware to engage and sustain student interest.

The use of digital multimedia could also assist in formative assessments. Project-based computer-assisted feedback is one way to provide students with the kind of information they need for mastery over time. In one school that the authors visited, students were using a video camera as they engaged in a science project to determine the rate at which an object falls. With time-lapse technology, these students were able to watch the rate of fall and calculate and recalculate the measurements until they were certain of both the answer and the manner in which they satisfied the answer. Students in another school, in Jefferson City, Missouri, were getting feedback on their writing by means of screen-casting technologies such as Jing or Screenr. Students would watch a Video of the Day, which was a short clip of something related to their learning. Students marveled at some of the videos made by people today. The videos shown were always ones that were found on teacher-approved and district-approved websites, such as TeacherTube or SchoolTube. Students then engaged in a time writing session, usually no more than 20 minutes, to deliver their thoughts on the video, relate it to their learning, or make predictions. Because this activity was designed more as an anticipatory set, students rarely received feedback on it immediately. Usually, the students would deliver their electronic journal into a teacher drop box. The teacher would then provide feedback using a screen-casting service and the students would follow along in their own individualized feedback response to their writing. The teacher would appear in a video and often "turn on" the students' papers through screen casting to guide them in their responses. This not only provided individualized attention for the student but focused on personalizing the learning for each child. The screencast would then be bundled in a link and the student could open his or her own link at a later time to watch the teacher review or critique their paper.

Here is another case of the use of emerging technologies in formative assessment strategies. In a small academy high school in Terre Haute, Indiana, students used clay animation to redesign several civil war battlefield scenes in a history class. They used a free software called Clay Animator to (literally) carve out details on the scenes they were producing. Student groups worked together, completing the project in small tasks. Each task was assigned and reviewed by peers, who then submitted feedback to the teacher. When students were done with their respective projects, several classes exchanged the videos they made and critiqued them, using well-crafted response sheets designed by the teacher. Students who provided open-ended feedback to other students had a more difficult time being objective or providing the necessary details needed to make feedback essential and meaningful. But generating a feedback response form by the teacher ensured that proper formative assessment could be given in a cooperative learning environment.

There are some challenges to the goal of sharing data across local and state systems. State data systems may not be compatible with those in districts of the same state. Lack of common interoperability standards could impede the smooth flow of data from statewide tests to individual schools. School administrators could look to the Common Data Standards (CDS) initiative for assistance in identifying and sharing key data sets between state departments of education and local education agencies. In 2010, Version 1.0 of the CDS was released (U.S. Department of Education, 2010). The issues of protecting student privacy in the release of data will be addressed in the section on the Family Educational Rights and Privacy Act (FERPA) of Chapter 6. Despite these limits, the effectiveness of educational programs should be evaluated through the sharing of student test data with key stakeholders in the public schools.

Embedded Assessment Technologies

Do you think that gaming has a place in the classroom? In NETP Goal 2.3, there is a call for "embedded assessment technologies, such as simulations, collaboration environments, virtual worlds, games and cognitive tutors in order to motivate today's digital-age learners" (U.S. Department of Education, 2010, p. 37). These interactive tools make learning more engaging for all types of students. Research is critical in order to keep up to date on how educational technology is working in the field. Simulation and gaming application in education have brought out new ways in which to learn. The field of robotics has provided additional opportunities for STEM course activities. The school leader must always look for new ways to explore and excite learning through the use of digital age communication and collaboration tools.

Gaming, for the most part, has been largely ignored or marginalized by schools despite the substantial efforts and research to support not only its popularity but also its benefits to students. Christensen et al. (2008) argue that virtual schooling is needed to help solve some of the problems in our traditional schools. Virtual schools are adopted by many district and state agencies primarily because of cost-cutting measures since most of these programs do have a cap on the total number of students enrolled. The Florida Virtual School system has shown that distance learning can play an important role in differentiated instruction.

This chapter has already explored some model practices in interactive multimedia for both formative and summative assessments. One further example of the power of emerging technologies in virtual learning environments is River City, a Harvard designed project funded by the National Science Foundation (NSF). In this learning environment, each middle school student becomes a data manipulating "avatar" in this scientific inquiry of life in an 18th-century city, where bacteria is being discovered and investigated (Dede, 2009; Dieterle, 2009). Students work individually and collaboratively to build their science competencies in this technologically enhanced interactive simulation.

Principled-Assessment Designs for Inquiry (PADI)

Are we assessing what's important in student learning? The fourth section of the NETP second goal (2.4) implores educators to use Universal Design for Learning (UDL) principles in order to assure that valid measurements of student learning occur. The NETP authors are concerned that traditional methods of assessment often do not measure what is important, because many conventional testing techniques evaluate skills extraneous to the task or competency. For instance, when learning a science concept, a student's ability to use word processing or to use a computer mouse should not be a focus of the test; rather, the understanding and application of the science concept should be measured.

As discussed in an earlier section of this chapter, UDL concepts also allow for technology-enhanced student assessments to be more accessible to diverse learners, especially those for whom English is a second language. English Language Learners and students with sight impairments are unfairly challenged by conventional testing formats because they are generally only formatted in English. The Principled-Assessment Designs for Inquiry (PADI) system is being used by some measurement designers to allow ELL and vision-impaired test-takers in their states to answer science assessment items (Zhang et al., 2010). By removing the need to know Standard English and the ability to see the questions, the PADI program is helping administrators to ensure that valid test measurements are applied to all students in their states or districts.

Assessment Data-Sharing

Although assessment data needs to be shared with key stakeholders in the education process, Goal 2.5 of the NETP is to make sure that student privacy is protected. Students over 18 years of age and parents or guardians of students under that age have the right to access student records, including assessment data; but there are some legal limits to that access by educators. School principals and superintendents should be aware that when data is aggregated across schools or districts information on individual student performance by name should not be available.

There are, therefore, some obstacles with which school administrators are faced in the sharing of student assessment data. Chapter 6 provides a further explanation of the Family Educational Rights and Privacy Act, the federal law which protects student privacy by prohibiting disclosure of personally identifiable information without prior written consent, unless the purpose is for administrators and teachers who have legitimate instructional roles. These are important concerns for principals and superintendents who must supervise the limited access to electronic learning records, including grade books and e-portfolios of student work.

TIPS FOR SCHOOL LEADERS

1 Realize the value of using social networking tools in meeting the learning needs of the iGeneration.

2 Understand that digital literacy is now media rich, including sound and screen, as well as interactive communication tools.

3 Consider implementing a one-to-one mobile learning initiative in your school or district.

4 Provide assessment-centered learning environments for more effective formative evaluations of student learning while it occurs.

5 Have a balanced assessment diet for students in your school or district with a mix of formative and summative evaluations.

6 Seek funding for the use of digital age tools in your school or district from technology-centered companies such as Dell and Verizon, or from federal subsidies for underserved students.

7 Allow for the differences between the ways in which digital natives and digital immigrants communicate in your school district.

8 Foster innovative instructional practices with emerging technology tools with the assistance of the school's technology coordinator.

9 Provide virtual or online course opportunities, especially in science, technology, engineering, and mathematics (STEM) areas, for students.

10 Encourage teachers to use interactive online programs to acquire free interactive lesson starters in their instruction.

11 Give students opportunities to use the latest presentation tools in order to create engaging content, such as Prezi or SlideShare slide shows or GoAnimate videos.

12 Motivate your students with constructivist applications of emerging technologies, such as augmented reality platforms.

13 Investigate the Universal Design for Learning (UDL) concept of making learning opportunities available to all students.

14 Prepare your students for STEM professions with the technologies described in this chapter.

15 Serve the needs of digitally excluded learners with more effective use of technologies for those students who are disabled, from rural areas, from low socio-economic areas, or from diverse cultures and languages.

16 Implement both formative and summative uses of new technology-based assessment tools.

17 Be cognizant of the Family Educational Rights and Privacy Act (FERPA), which limits the sharing of student assessment data.

18 Consider applying these Golden Rules for Teaching with Technology:

(a) Good teaching matters. The design of learning activities of quality is important for all delivery methods. Each medium has its own aesthetic; therefore, professional design is important.

(b) There is no super-technology. Each has its strengths and weaknesses. An integrated mix of technologies is most effective. In addition to new media-rich technologies, these four media should still be available for teachers and learners: print, audio, television, and computers with high-speed Internet access.

(c) Balance variety with economy. Using many technologies makes design more complex and expensive. New technologies are not necessarily better than old ones. Limit the range of technologies in any given learning activity.

(d) Teamwork and student interaction are essential in traditional and virtual learning situations. No one person has all the skills to develop and deliver effective distance learning. Subject matter experts, instructional designers, and media specialists are key to online course success.

(e) Teachers need training to use technology effectively. Professional development is critical. The choice of medium will depend greatly upon the number of learners reached over the life of a course.

(f) How and what learners learn is the goal of instruction, and technology is one tool. Learning is essential, but so is the thinking process. Technology, if used wisely, enhances students' cognitive development and problem-solving skills.

Summary

A thorough discussion of emerging technologies appropriate to the instruction and assessment of iGeneration learners has been presented. At the beginning of this chapter, two senior directors of technology, one in California and the other in Georgia, reflect on the value of creating "a digital learning culture" with a "one-to-one mobile learning initiative" that will promote the "reinvention of curriculum, teaching, and assessment" and a "Balanced Assessment Diet" for consideration by school superintendents, technology coordinators, and principals.

By implementing the new assessment initiatives described in this chapter, program directors, principals, and superintendents can become better data-based decision-makers when it comes to student learning. However, assessment is more than measuring student performance on state tests; it is also about measuring the 21st-century problem-solving skills and applying knowledge to real-life settings in a more networked global society and economy.

After reading the chapter and completing the needs assessment survey, the reader should be able to analyze his or her own school district in order to determine if there are technology-rich, learner-centered classroom environments. If so, then you, as an educational leader, should also find out if teachers in your schools are using digital-age instructional techniques that best meet the needs of the diverse learners of your learning community. For example, technology tools can enhance differentiated instructional methods to assist disabled learners. Emerging technology software is also used by Professional Learning Communities (PLCs) to align state standards across the curriculum and to promote higher-order thinking skills for students. This chapter supplements ideas on how to implement NETS.A Standard 2 of providing a "digital-age learning culture" with the NETP goals of enhancing instruction and assessment. The authors give examples of best practices in the use of newer mobile access devices in flexible and media-rich learning environments. In the next chapter, school leaders will discover how to supervise and provide professional development for teachers who should be using these digital age instructional tools.

School administrators who rate themselves and their schools or districts with scores of 5 and 4 are already meeting the standards indicated in those items. Ratings of 1 or 2 would indicate areas of needed professional growth by either the school district, or the school leader, or both in order to meet the NETS.A standards or NETP goals.

TABLE 2.1 School Administrator's Technology Leadership Self-Assessment Survey: Leading Instruction with New Technologies (Chapter 2)

Directions: Please respond to each item by circling a number from 1 to 5, where 5 = strongly agree; 4 = agree; 3 = neutral; 2 = disagree; 1 = strongly disagree.

This survey is based on National Education Technology Plan (NETP) Goals 1 and 2 (NETP 1.0 to 1.4 and NETP 2.0 to 2.5) and National Educational Technology Standards and Performance Indicators for Administrators (NETS.A) Standard 2 (NETS. A 2.a, 2.b, 2.c, 2.d, 2.e).

5 = strongly agree (SA); 4 = agree (A); 3 = neutral (N); 2 = disagree (D); 1 = strongly disagree (SD)	SA	A	N	D	SD
1 I empower students to be meaningful participants in a globally networked society (NETP 1.0).	5	4	3	2	1
2 I encourage my state's department of education to use technology in implementing standards in all content areas (NETP 1.1).	5	4	3	2	1
3 Universal Design for Learning (UDL) principles are the basis for technology-based learning resources (NETP 1.2).	5	4	3	2	1
4 I support the availability of online and blended online/in-class courses for all students (NETP 1.3).	5	4	3	2	1
5 I encourage the use of digital age tools to improve the science, technology, engineering, and mathematics (STEM) skills of all students in my school or district (NETP 1.4).	5	4	3	2	1
6 In our district or school, we assess "what matters" in order to improve instruction (NETP 2.0).	5	4	3	2	1
7 In our district or school, assessment data is used to give "timely and actionable" feedback on student performance (NETP 2.1).	5	4	3	2	1
8 We use technology in our school or district to improve both formative and summative assessments (NETP 2.2).	5	4	3	2	1
9 In order to motivate learners in our school(s), we use "embedded assessment technologies," (NETP 2.3) such as:					
(a) simulations;	5	4	3	2	1
(b) virtual worlds;	5	4	3	2	1
(c) augmented realities;	5	4	3	2	1
(d) gaming;	5	4	3	2	1
(e) cognitive tutors;	5	4	3	2	1
(f) online collaborations.	5	4	3	2	1

5 = strongly agree (SA); 4 = agree (A); 3 = neutral (N); 2 = disagree (D); 1 = strongly disagree (SD)	SA	A	N	D	SD
10 Universal Design for Learning (UDL) principles are the basis for many assessments of what all students need to learn (NETP 2.4).	5	4	3	2	1
11 Student privacy is ensured when assessment data is shared with key stakeholders in order to improve learning (NETP 2.5).	5	4	3	2	1
12 I empower my teacher colleagues to take risks with technology in order to improve instruction (NETS.A 2.a)	5	4	3	2	1
13 As I model the use of emerging technologies in my school or district, I also promote their use in learning (NETS.A 2.b).	5	4	3	2	1
14 Instruction in our school or district is enhanced by advances in technology in order for it to be (NETS.A 2.c):					
(a) learner centered;	5	4	3	2	1
(b) differentiated;	5	4	3	2	1
(c) fully accessed by special education students;	5	4	3	2	1
(d) fully accessed by students in rural areas;	5	4	3	2	1
(e) fully accessed by students in low socio-economic households;	5	4	3	2	1
(f) fully accessed by English language learners (ELLs);	5	4	3	2	1
(g) fully accessed by gifted students.	5	4	3	2	1
15 I ensure that new technologies are researched and implemented where appropriate across the curriculum (NETS.A 2.d).	5	4	3	2	1
16 I practice digital age collaboration by participating in professional online learning communities (NETS.A 2.e):					
(a) locally;	5	4	3	2	1
(b) statewide;	5	4	3	2	1
(c) nationally;	5	4	3	2	1
(d) globally.	5	4	3	2	1

V. E. Garland and C. Tadeja, 2012

DISCUSSION QUESTIONS

1 What are some ways in which administrators within your own school site or district can support both the integration of technology in instruction and more learner-centered environments?

2 How can professional development be embedded within the contractual school day in order to provide teacher training in new technologies?

3 Think about how you use technology in your own learning and professional growth. Then reflect on how students use the same or different technologies in their social networking. How might teachers harness the "digital age culture" of the new generation? Create a visual chart to illustrate the differences between digital immigrants and digital natives. Discuss your chart in a group or with a partner.

4 How can student achievement levels and problem-solving skills in science, technology, engineering, and mathematics (STEM) subject matters be enhanced with web-based digital tools?

5 Why should assessment of student performance be both formative and summative? In what ways can school administrators be advocates for "measuring what matters" in your school or district?

6 Analyze the online learning opportunities available to students in your school or district. Include a discussion of "marginalized learners" and their access to distance learning networks.

7 At the beginning of Chapter 2, Karen Connaghan reflects on the value of creating "a digital learning culture" with a "one-to-one mobile learning initiative." Discuss the availability of Internet access devices to students in your school or district. How might the access to mobile technology devices by all students cause "reinvention of curriculum, teaching, and assessment" practices?

8 In her leader reflection, Jill Hobson refers to a "Balanced Assessment Diet" and poses the question: "If you were putting the one-time-a-year standardized test on one side of a scale and classroom assessments on the other, which side should weigh more?" Please answer this question in terms of the value you place on standardized tests, as opposed to more "authentic" types of assessments. What might be the roles of digital age tools in both types of assessment?

9 Based on your responses to the self-assessment for Chapter 2, what are the next steps you might take in more effective leadership of instruction with new technologies in your school or district? What technology resources would you need in your own professional e-portfolio in order to assist you in achieving your goals?

3
Teacher Supervision and Professional Development

Synopsis

How are digital age tools used by school administrators in supervising teachers? What are best practices in professional opportunities to improve both leaders and teachers in their use of emerging technologies? This chapter explores current trends in observing teachers and in providing technology integration opportunities for all educators and stakeholders in the learning process, including students and their parents. Professional development can be in the form of in-service days, workshops, conferences, online professional learning communities, and more. School principals, program directors, and superintendents all play a vital role in not only modeling the effective use of technology but also supporting and encouraging training in digital age tools.

Reflections of the Former Student Dean at a Maine High School

While many may have scoffed at the use of technology in the classroom and would prefer we stick with the three "Rs" [reading, writing, and arithmetic], we have found that, by embracing these technological naysayers and encouraging them to come into the building and get "hands-on" with various forms of technology, they begin to see its true potential. Three years ago we became part of a statewide initiative to provide each high school student with his or her own laptop for the school year. While we knew students would be very eager to get their laptops, we also knew that the faculty and the parents would be less enthusiastic. In order to assist our faculty with the transition from a more traditional pen and paper classroom and grade book to a fully supported online student information system, we provided professional development during the school day and offered various groups of teachers off-site trainings and visits with other schools that were already living completely in the digital world.

For the parents of our students, we knew we had to present them with a clear message and rationale on why their children were being given laptops. In order to help communicate our message to them, we invited all parents into the school and put a laptop in their hands and helped them learn all about the programs and the potential these machines offered to them and their own kids. We knew we were going to have to change the culture concerning how people thought about technology; and we thought that this technology training for parents was a great way to start that change. Over the years, incoming students' parents now expect these workshops and are often taught or assisted by more veteran parents. The culture change of embracing technology as an effective tool, not only for their children in the classrooms but also for the parents themselves, is beginning to take place all across our district.

Once all stakeholders see the potential benefits of embracing technology, be it in the classroom for an increased capacity for teaching and learning, or at home where students are exploring more on their own to become more connected individuals, only then will the endless possibilities technology gives us become evident. While the cultural change is never smooth and simple (there will be bumps, seen and unseen, along the way), there must also be a dedication and perseverance to the utilization of technology within the school in order for it to succeed.

Andrew K. Korman was the dean of students at one of the nation's Coalition of Essential Schools, Noble High School in North Berwick, Maine. He is now an Assistant Principal of Gloucester High School in Massachusetts. He is a doctoral student at the University of New Hampshire, studying leadership and policy development with a focus on male high school dropouts.

Introduction

With administrator support in the training of teachers and parents, digital age tools can provide the new, exciting, and effective learning culture for students that is described in the previous chapter. The leader reflection from a high school administrator in a state which has a one laptop per student initiative introduces this chapter's focus on teacher development, as well as on student and parent collaboration in learning new technologies. In addition to reviewing the value of varied professional development opportunities, the chapter explores such emerging technologies as "bug-in-the-ear" for teacher supervision and iEtherPad for conducting interactive staff meetings. An enhanced discussion of the networking tools described in Chapter 2 will show how teachers can make connections with other teachers in the field. Expanded analysis is made of the use of cell phones and Poll Everywhere applications, which have real-time features that allow greater participatory decision-making.

Teacher Supervision in the Digital Age

What digital age technology tools are used in observing classrooms in your school or district? With permission from teachers and students and their parents, exemplary lessons can be filmed and made available to the entire staff through online streaming videos. Individual lessons that might need improvement could also be videotaped and analyzed in a one-on-one post-observation conference. Peer coaching, without the threat of evaluation, could also incorporate filmed lessons either on or offline. In conducting observations of teachers, many principals and other supervisors are using specialized applications on touch tablets, such as the iPad2, for collecting and sharing data on student and teacher performance in the classroom. However, it is important for school leaders to link any teacher supervision and evaluation system to the school district's mission statement and technology plan. Since some teachers are unaware of the teacher evaluation criteria in their districts, they should be involved in the process of designing and implementing any new observation techniques.

One new product that involves data collection of classroom observations is Teachscape Walk. It is a handheld wireless device that serves as a reporting system for administrative walkthroughs and is based on a seven-stage classroom observation process. The supervisor who uses Teachscape should be trained on how to translate data into practical action steps for the teacher to improve instruction (http://www. teachscape.com/products/walkthrough). In order to be effective in the use of Teachscape Walk, the educational leader should commit to a collaborative process of providing the teacher with data that would be helpful to improve student engagement and learning.

Another approach to digital age supervision is virtual coaching, also referred to as "bug-in-the-ear" technology. Through an earpiece, teachers receive real-time feedback from a virtual coach as they teach. The observer can use Skype to see the lesson and to intervene with suggestions for improved instructional strategies while the lesson unfolds (Rock et al., 2011). This is a collaborative, synchronous method of the supervisor directly suggesting to the teacher ways of improving lessons as they occur.

Classroom observation data can be useful in determining the professional development needs of teachers in their use of emerging technologies. Almost all teachers are required to conduct yearly goal setting, and most tenured teachers have self-directed growth plans. In the increasing number of districts that require student e-portfolios, teachers are also encouraged or mandated to have e-portfolios of their professional work. In addition to the classroom observation data, the artifacts provided in the teacher e-portfolios can be strong indicators of their use of digital age tools. For instance, does the eighth-grade social studies teacher require students to give content presentations of their projects on the Civil War with Prezi or SlideRocket software programs? Professional opportunities for teachers to gain confidence and skills in using such applications are discussed in the next section.

Teaching: Prepare and Connect

Technology cannot survive in schools without full integration in professional practice by all educators, and that must both include and be led by educational administrators (Garland, 2010a). The teacher is already plagued with numerous tasks that can be cumbersome to the primary task of instruction. School districts generally have personnel who either have a background in technology or have access to instructional technology experts. A model school can act as a repository for ideas or resources on the latest and greatest uses in educational technology. There have been times where supervisors have conducted classroom walk-throughs in which they learned something new about the teachers' use of technology. Administrators can look around at their own school sites and find ways to provide students and teachers with access to connected learning. School principals, technology coordinators, and central office administrators thus have a key role in providing meaningful technology in-service activities in order to train, retain, and reduce the isolation of teachers and other student support staff members. This is the basis of NETP Goal 3: "Teaching: Prepare and Connect":

> 3.0 Teaching: Professional educators will be supported individually and in teams by technology that connects them to data, content, resources, expertise, and learning experiences that enable and inspire more effective teaching for all learners.
>
> 3.1 Expand opportunities for educators to have access to technology-based content, resources, and tools where and when they need them.
>
> 3.2 Leverage social networking technologies and platforms to create communities of practice that provide career-long personal learning opportunities for educators within and across schools, pre-service preparation and in-service educational institutions, and professional organizations.
>
> 3.3 Use technology to provide all learners with online access to effective teaching and better learning opportunities and options in places where they are not otherwise available and in blended (online and offline) learning environments.
>
> 3.4 Provide pre-service and in-service educators with professional learning experiences powered by technology to increase their digital literacy and enable them to create compelling assignments for students that improve learning, assessment, and instructional practices.
>
> 3.5. Develop a teaching force skilled in online instruction.
> (U.S. Department of Education, 2010, pp. 47–48)

While conducting research for this textbook, the authors spoke to practicing educators across the nation. Many teachers complained that the unavailability of contracted time during the school day for professional development activities is a primary reason for the lack of their technology expertise. However, administrators should take note that teachers' professional development does not have to take a great deal of time. In fact, some principals told the authors that they committed no more than five minutes in their weekly faculty meetings to explaining a new web-teaching tool to their teachers. The administrators who use this collaborative approach found it to be both fun and easy. There are undoubtedly hundreds of new Web 2.0 tools out there now on the Internet just waiting to be explored. Staff members can research one or a few and report back their findings. Tools that are particularly helpful are those that help to strengthen communication or collaboration. In the previous chapter, we discussed the importance of using these Web 2.0 tools because they are favored by the iGeneration of learners. Here is a review of the differences between Web 1.0 and Web 2.0: Whereas Web 1.0 has 45 million users, Web 2.0 now has over 1 billion global users. Another key distinction is that Web 2.0 is free, web based, and open source. On the other hand, Web 1.0 is proprietary, based on licensed or purchased applications.

There is a new educational discussion about the term Web 3.0, or the "Semantic Web," a term which was coined by Tim Berners-Lee, also the inventor of the first World Wide Web. The belief is that Web 3.0 will have technology capable of reinventing the online world. For instance, instead of going on your browser now to look for multiple searches on where to catch a movie and a great local restaurant afterwards, a Web 3.0 search will analyze the request and not only provide a slew of answers but also organize it for you. In other words, Web 3.0 is more of a "personal portable web" for users. It has great potential for teaching. Imagine how easily students might be able to research primary sources in social studies, or analyze factors causing global warming using Web 3.0!

Professional Development in the Digital Age

Do teachers really like the professional development activities your school district provides for them? Effective professional development is needed to replace the outdated and ineffective past practices of "top-down," "one-shot," "sit-and-get" workshops performed by outside experts. Astonishingly, half of all new teachers leave the profession in their first five years (Nolan and Hoover, 2011). Many have not had the pre-service teacher training preparation or the in-service professional development that ensures success in the real-life classroom, such as the integration of technology tools in instruction. Not only the "digital immigrant" veteran teachers and administrators but also the "digital native" younger teachers and administrators need to be prepared to use digital age technology in their practice.

School principals, in particular, need to understand and facilitate collaborative models of professional development. The delivery of in-service programs for teachers should be interactive and ongoing. The content should address the 21st-century educational mandates for competency-based instruction and connected learning (Garland, 2008). Administrators and teachers alike need to engage in career-long learning networks. Professional development opportunities with technology-enhanced environments include online or blended online/offline courses, online Professional Learning Communities (PLCs), and the use of web-based resources such as sample lessons or educational experts.

In their own professional development efforts, administrators themselves must learn the technology that best applies to their profession. As described more extensively in the next chapter, school leaders need in-service training in order to participate in technology planning, funding, and purchasing. They are also responsible for supervising, recognizing, and evaluating teachers' use of technology to enhance instruction and improve learning.

Networked Professional Learning Communities

Educators need to have both training and 24/7 access to instructional resources and student-related data systems (NETP Goal 3.1). The connected teaching model presented in Chapter 2 gives teachers and administrators the ability to align student learning information with appropriate instructional resources. PLCs enhance the collaboration between school principals and teachers in improving student learning. In the connected teaching model, administrators support teachers in transitioning from teacher-centered to more student-centered instruction (Garland, 2011). Teachers have new roles as facilitators of self-directed student learning. Networked communities can enhance teachers' and students' access to content, experts, and peer collaboration. These online learning opportunities can be within a school, between schools and homes, among schools, or between schools and community resources such as museums. Therefore, there are no limits on where or when one teaches or learns, whether collaboratively or individually.

Another exemplary model of a professional learning community is Math Forum, sponsored by the School of Education at Drexel University. According to the Math Forum website, it is an online resource which has been assisting teachers, students, parents, educational researchers, and mathematicians for the past 20 years. The goal of Math Forum is to improve student learning in mathematics by providing educators with online mentoring and professional development. Students can access math problems and puzzles, and educators can share ideas and acquire new teaching skills (http://mathforum.org). Higher education professors in teacher training institutes are already finding Math Forum helpful in pre-service teacher preparation in mathematics. They are using a "Problem of the Week" feature to give pre-service teachers practice in giving feedback to middle school students who are trying to solve this mathematical problem (U.S. Department of Education, 2010).

Administrators should consider purchasing selective subscription-based online services, such as Math Forum, in order to improve the professional training for teachers of all subjects and grade levels. It is not enough that students are actively engaged with the technologies used by "tech savvy" teachers in only one or two courses in the school, and yet are passive learners in the other classrooms. Students deserve to have teachers with high expectations and engaging activities in all their courses. In the next section, we explore how the teaching of online courses can be improved.

Teacher Training in Online Instruction

The concluding section (3.5) of NETP Goal 3 is to have all current and future teachers trained in online instruction. This national mandate was reconfirmed in a recent jobs creation federal initiative. The federal executive branch called for high-speed Internet in all our nation's schools and an increase in a technologically "savvy" teaching force. Because online learning has become key in higher education and increasingly more important in pre K-12 public schools, educators are learning how to blend best practices in instructional design with emerging technologies in virtual course offerings. Both online and hybrid on/off line courses are becoming more interactive, with opportunities to individualize instruction for diverse learning styles (Garland, 2010b). Adaptive technologies to meet the needs of disabled learners are also constantly changing and improving.

Some states are establishing standards for online courses. More teacher preparation institutions of higher learning have online teacher certification programs in order to meet the state standards. The University of La Verne in California and Concordia University in Illinois offer either voluntary or mandatory certification for teaching online modules. Developing a teaching force skilled in online teaching addresses the needs of the new iGeneration learners. But preparing to teach online is more than just a certification issue. Teachers and administrators need to be constantly trained and certain competencies need to be achieved within the course of training (Connecticut Department of Higher Education, 2011). Online teaching strategies also need to be examined for their effectiveness.

The School Administrator as Technology Leader in Professional Development

You have read how the administrators in one Maine school district provide professional development for their teachers, students, and parents with effective technologies, while they themselves are using those same digital tools. In this section, you will find additional cases in which school leaders model the effective use of new technologies in their own practice. A technology director in upstate New York has been praised for her use of technology during the course of the workday. She has been seen using her smartphone to access her meeting schedule via a real-time calendar system for the week. In meetings, she has been noted to use presentation tools such as SlideShare and Prezi directly from her laptop to display a presentation. During outings, she has been using blogging tools, such as Edmodo.com and Ning.com, to keep in touch with community members.

In another recent case, a principal of a technology high school in Baton Rouge, Louisiana, made a change in her modes of presenting information in staff development meetings. She noticed that students were becoming more "tech savvy" than their teachers in this designated technology school. The principal decided that she would take one Friday each month and dedicate it to getting the professional staff more immersed in the digital age in the hopes of their keeping up with the technologies that the students were using. Each of these Fridays was filled with presentations from various teachers about a new technology device, the use of cloudware, or other "apps" that are widely available to the public. The only caveat was that each new application had to have some kind of connection to learning or teaching. At other times, this principal would invite guest speakers such as the district technology coordinator or a professor of a local college to come in and show her staff how to use digital age tools to propel student learning. Or she would simply have the staff take 20 minutes to discover something on the Internet to share with others. This innovative, risk-taking leader discovered that her new strategies for collaborating worked well in the future monthly staff meetings. Furthermore, her approach seemed to have increased her staff's morale and technology awareness. They were now more easily able to relate to students' use of technology and even share new things with them. This did not interfere with district or state benchmarks because the focus remained on using or discovering technology that could help with learning or teaching. The age-old adage of why have a meeting when most of the information can be transmitted via a memo rang true for this principal. Instead of holding weekly meetings for the sake of holding meetings, she decided that she would dedicate one year of monthly staff meetings, all focused on technology enhancements in education, to having the staff of this technology high school be more immersed in the digital age.

Here are two additional scenarios of principals who used emerging technologies in staff meetings. A school principal in Austin, Texas, wanted his teachers to give him feedback on students' scores on a recent test. He did this using Poll Everywhere, a web-based application that gathers live responses in meetings, conferences, or classrooms, such as those at the Massachusetts Institute of Technology. According to the Poll Everywhere website, it is a popular site used globally through texting or Twitter (http://www.polleverywhere.com/). The principal in this case used Poll Everywhere on his smartphone at a staff meeting in order to take a live survey of how his staff felt about the recent scores. Instead of openly asking his staff of about 100 their opinions of the scores, with the expectation of only receiving a handful of responses, he used Poll Everywhere to get almost 100% of those in attendance to give their take on the scores recently published. The website offered the principal the chance to take a real-time live poll of his staff and translate it into meaningful data. It is important that site administrators model technologies that can chart school progress with data-driven decision-making tools such as those offered on these websites.

In the next case, a principal in Manhattan, Kansas, utilized iEtherPad in teacher teams to create and refine lessons online. In a recent professional development, both the principal and her teachers logged into iEtherPad.com. This is a free service that allows multiple users the opportunity to collaborate in real time. The principal puts up a question onto the shared iEtherPad and instructs the teachers to respond to it. Instantly, the teachers can share their responses to both the principal and other teachers, and all can see each other's responses. The principal noticed that many of her teachers were visual learners and the use of the iEtherPad allowed all of them to get a visual response to the question or idea presented. The principal was so impressed with their responses with the iEtherPad that she printed the teachers' input and now uses this device to show parents, district officials, and other visitors this powerful use of online collaboration. iEtherPad is now a common tool used in all of her staff meetings.

These cases are examples of how school administrators can model the effective use of digital age tools in their own practice. It is not enough to talk about and be mesmerized by the latest technology tools out there. They must be utilized in a way where people in the community, teachers, and other leaders alike see their school leaders talk about technology and, more importantly, use it effectively to improve student learning.

Blogging as Professional Development

It is essential for school leaders to participate in local, national, and global learning initiatives in order to stimulate educational creativity and digital age collaboration. One way to do this is through the use of blogs. Blogging allows participants to share different perspectives and enables individuals to gather information and export ideas (Young et al., 2011). Since there are literally thousands of blogs on the web, perhaps one way to start is small. A local website within the district can host blogs for teachers. The blogs can be extended in order to allow parents, administrators, school board members, and even students the chance to add to existing blogs. There are numerous principals and superintendents, such as Principal William Carozza and Superintendent Steven Chamberlin of the Hopkinton School District in New Hampshire, who comment on their use of blogs in the leader reflection in the next chapter. These educational leaders utilize blogs regularly in one way or another to disseminate information or to begin a discussion on some element in education within the district itself.

Conferences as Professional Development

In order to ensure effective practices in the infusion of technology across the disciplines, professional development opportunities do not have to occur within the boundaries of a particular school or district. There are numerous conferences, both online and on-ground, that provide training for teachers in emerging technologies. A principal or superintendent can never fall short in having technology opportunities afforded to his or her teachers. A "digital native" experiences many technologies earlier than a "digital immigrant." Therefore, it is important to let teachers explore what is out there and connect with other educators who have proven success with technology.

Superintendents, principals, program coordinators, and technology coordinators can stay connected by participating in annual conventions and conferences in which digital age collaborations are celebrated. Educational administrators can now join some of these online in interactive environments such as webinars that are as meaningful as those they attend in person. One highly touted conference, Technology, Entertainment, Design (TED), is an excellent venue that produces two annual conferences which highlight the latest in innovation, thinking, and technology. TED leverages its conferences by offering well-known speakers, who are only given 18 minutes or less to present their ideas. TED organizers have found that 18 minutes is the average attention span of participants. Notable speakers have included Bill Gates, Bill Clinton, Al Gore, Paul Simon, Sir Richard Branson, Bono, and others. Other conferences similar to TED include the Good Experience Live (GEL), and the Entertainment Gathering (EG) conference. The latest technologies and innovations are presented from some of the premier leaders in their fields at these conferences.

Many school districts do not have the resources to cover costs associated with the participation of their professional staff in some of these out-of-district conferences. However, the school administrator does not have to attend a groundbreaking conference in order to understand how to become a more effective educational technology leader. A technology coordinator, for instance, may find ways to design a digital age partnership with other educational leaders, such as the collaborative-based websites Keypals, TeacherTube, Online mentoring, and the Open Source Initiative (OSI). The educational leader is thus urged to attend an online or local technology conference in order to better stimulate innovation at the school or district level.

TIPS FOR SCHOOL LEADERS

1 Vary the types of professional development opportunities; they can be in-service days, workshops, conferences, and online Professional Learning Communities.

2 Consider technology training for parents of students in your school district, especially if you have a one-on-one laptop initiative.

3 Try such emerging technologies as "bug-in-the-ear" for teacher supervision and real-time collaborative tools for conducting interactive staff meetings.

4 For greater teacher participation in decision-making, use Poll Everywhere.

5 Use emerging technologies for more effective observations of instruction,

including new "apps" on the iPad or new data collection programs such as Teachscape Walk.

6 Use five minutes in faculty meetings to have those who use Web 2.0 tools explain how they can be used to engage the iGeneration of learners.

7 Be aware of the differing needs of both the "digital immigrant" veteran teachers and administrators, and the more "digital native" younger teachers or administrators.

8 Provide professional development opportunities with technology-enhanced environments, including online or blended online/offline courses and online Professional Learning Communities.

9 Encourage teachers to assign user-generated content in which students apply blogs, wikis, and other social networking tools in learning activities.

10 Give your mathematics teachers professional development with online mentoring programs such as Math Forum in order to improve student learning in one of the key science, technology, engineering, and mathematics (STEM) subject areas.

11 Determine if your state has standards for the teaching of online courses and if you should encourage the teachers of hybrid or online classes in your school district to complete any certification programs that meet those state standards.

12 Model the effective use of emerging technologies in your own practice by using such digital age tools as managerial "apps" on your smartphone or new presentation and communication tools on your laptop.

13 Look up real-time collaboration technologies, such as a search on the Internet for "real-time collaborative pads" to investigate ways to use in teacher teams and refine lessons online.

14 Host a local website within your school district for blogging with students, teachers, parents, administrators, school board members, and community members.

15 Stimulate innovation by participating in an online or local technology conference.

Summary

Because school principals, program directors, and superintendents are always observing, supervising, and evaluating teachers, they have the opportunity to ascertain what types of professional development are needed to improve instruction in their own buildings or districts. In this chapter, the authors apply NETP Goal 3 in order to ensure that teachers have professional development opportunities for the effective use of technology in instruction. In addition to using web-based tools such as Poll Everywhere in their own schools, principals and other educational leaders can use online professional communities for professional development opportunities. In the next chapter, the importance of creating an effective technology infrastructure to further ensure excellence in professional practice is explored.

School administrators who rate themselves and their schools or districts with scores of 5 and 4 are already meeting the standards indicated in those items. Ratings of 1 or 2 would indicate areas of needed professional growth by either the school district, or the school leader, or both in order to meet the NETS.A standards or NETP goals.

TABLE 3.1 School Administrator's Technology Leadership Self-Assessment Survey: Teacher Supervision and Professional Development (Chapter 3)

Directions: Please respond to each item by circling a number from 1 to 5, where 5 = strongly agree; 4 = agree; 3 = neutral; 2 = disagree; 1 = strongly disagree.

This survey is based on National Education Technology Plan (NETP) Goal 3 (NETP 3.0 to 3.5).

5 = strongly agree (SA); 4 = agree (A); 3 = neutral (N); 2 = disagree (D); 1 = strongly disagree (SD)	SA	A	N	D	SD
1 Teachers in my school(s) are fully supported by professional development in technology which meets both individual and collaborative purposes (NETP 3.0).	5	4	3	2	1
2 Educators in my school(s) have full "24/7" access to technology tools (NETP 3.1).	5	4	3	2	1
3 Social networking tools are applied to effective instructional practices in my school(s) (NETP 3.2).	5	4	3	2	1
4 Online and blended online/offline learning environments are available to all learners in my school(s) (NETP 3.3).	5	4	3	2	1
5 Professional development in digital literacy for improved instruction and student assessment is provided for all teachers in my school(s) (NETP 3.4).	5	4	3	2	1
6 Teachers in my school(s) are trained in effective online instructional techniques (NETP 3.5).	5	4	3	2	1

V. E. Garland and C. Tadeja, 2012

DISCUSSION QUESTIONS

1 In the leader reflection piece for this chapter, Andrew Korman, former dean of students at Maine's Noble High School, current Assistant Principal at Massachusett's Gloucester High School, concludes: "While the cultural change is never smooth and simple (there will be bumps, seen and unseen, along the way), there must also be a dedication and perseverance to the utilization of technology within the school in order for it to succeed." Explain how you might successfully meet the challenges ahead in the "cultural change" to the use of digital age tools in your school or district.

2 The authors give several examples of the use of emerging technologies for conducting classroom observations, ranging from the use of customized applications on smartphones to the implementation of Teachscape Walk and "bug-in-the-ear" devices. Discuss how you would compare these classroom data collection techniques with the ones you are currently using in your supervisory practices.

3 How might you improve the professional development opportunities in the use of emerging technologies for teachers and administrators in your school or district? Describe the circumstances in which you might encourage teachers or administrators to participate in online mentoring programs or networked Professional Learning Communities.

4 What are the challenges in teaching online or hybrid online courses? Does your state have certification requirements for distance-learning teachers? If so, how effective are the programs that certify those teachers? Analyze how specific obstacles to "cyber classes" can be met, such as student isolation or the lack of face-to-face interactions.

5 How do you model the effective use of emerging technologies in your own practice, such as in conducting staff meetings or in communicating with teachers and parents?

6 Based on your responses to the self-assessment for Chapter 3, what are the next steps you might take in more effective teacher observations or greater professional development opportunities in your school or district? What technology resources would you need in your own professional e-portfolio in order to assist you in achieving your goals?

4

The Technology Infrastructure

Synopsis

This chapter focuses on how the school administrator implements NETS.A Standard 3 and NETP Goal 4. The third ISTE NETS.A standard describes how the school leader can use digital age tools to achieve excellence in his or her professional practice. NETP Goal 4 urges the school administrator to create technology-enhanced school district infrastructure, with appropriate access to data for students, educators, and parents/guardians. In addition to modeling the effective uses of technology, the school leader must support teachers and other stakeholders in using technology resources for school improvement. The stakeholders in these school improvement efforts need to have access to databases and management systems, which facilitate communication and collaboration between teachers and students or parents, as well as between administrators and parents.

In this chapter, the principal and the superintendent are encouraged to engage in educational technology research and to use communication tools which support the digital age of leading. The following leader reflection is a collaborative effort between a principal and a superintendent in the same school district. The reader should note which emerging technologies these administrators consider to be effective in engaging students to learn and in communicating with parents.

Reflections of a New Hampshire Superintendent and Principal

Time, tools, and training – three critical, inextricably linked concepts, necessary to move a school district forward. As technology becomes more and more interwoven into the fabric of everyday life, schools need to provide the time, tools, and training to utilize technology to improve the efficiency and effectiveness of all aspects of schooling. At the same time, schools must be careful not to replace core practices with technological replacements simply because they are less expensive or the next big thing. Successfully implementing technological improvements with efficacy to a school district's core mission and values is the land of critical mass. It is the noble pursuit in the Hopkinton School District.

From the district perspective, technology has been interwoven into every aspect of district operations.

Communication: From community and parent email listservs, to wiki websites used to track and receive feedback on committee work, to screencasts that allow particular nuances of a subject to be explained, to posting school board audio recordings on the website, to an automatic call system: technology has enhanced communication with the community.

Collaboration: From utilizing Google documents to develop a policy, technology plan, or project work to document sharing with the executive assistant, to Skyping in an administrator home with an ill child to a meeting, technology has enhanced collaboration.

Operations: From a budget program that supports off-site purchase order approval and easy report production, to a professional development management tool which tracks activities by goal, to the approval, tracking, and revision of federal grant monies: web-based applications have increased operational efficiency exponentially.

Data-based decision-making: From gap analyses by subgroup on the state test, to high-quality self-adjusting assessments, to understanding each student's Lexile to support reading selection, to making just-in-time student information available to focus intervention planning: technology has enhanced the past practice of decision by anecdote by including data.

From a school perspective, it is important that we utilize technology to force greater efficiency. Technology must do more than raise the bar for our work; it has to create time so that we can be more effective and have more time for instruction. *Teaching is still a contact sport.*

With a relatively simple technology infrastructure, principals complete classroom observations with laptops and iPads and feedback is sent instantly to the teacher via email. While deeper conversations must still occur face to face, teachers and administrators can exchange details such as schedules and meeting minutes via email with important faculty documents housed on a wiki. Instead of staff meetings dominated by minutiae, technology is used to communicate everything that doesn't need discussion so that staff meetings can be primarily utilized for professional development.

Parent communication has reached the 21st century in Hopkinton. Harold Martin School completes a monthly podcast for parents utilizing a new digital media studio funded primarily through grant funds. While led primarily by the principal, the podcast includes contributions from students and teachers. Parents feel more connected via a podcast versus the traditional weekly newsletter sent home in student backpacks. One school utilizes a Twitter account to remind parents of timely information.

Classrooms throughout the district utilize interactive white boards, which have begun to revolutionize feedback of content understanding between the student and teacher. Through interactive Quick Response systems, students are able to quickly inform the teacher on their level of understanding of a particular concept. It seems unfathomable that we ever taught geometry without this incredible tool. Even the primary grade teachers are beginning to utilize laptops and computer projector technology, which allows them to conjure up a thought and be able to express it through the wide range of the Internet.

Want to take a course that is not offered in your school, such as a higher-level calculus class or a world language such as Mandarin Chinese? One can utilize a *virtual school* such as our own in New Hampshire called Virtual Learning Academy Charter School. While the offices for VLACS are located in Exeter, the *school* is located wherever a computer, tablet, or smartphone device and a wireless connection exist.

Time is the currency of school improvement. Technology has the power to simultaneously improve all aspects of schooling while forcing increased efficiency. The increasing efficiency allows more time to focus on the leadership and substantive change. However, it is essential that technology be seen as a tool that exists to serve the educational values we hold dear. It can never be an entity unto itself.

William V. Carozza is the principal of the Harold Martin School in Hopkinton, New Hampshire, and a nationally known digital age technology user of social networking tools for educational communications and improvement.

Steven M. Chamberlin is the superintendent of schools in Hopkinton School District and a doctoral student at the University of New Hampshire, studying leadership and policy development.

Introduction

In the reflection piece from the New Hampshire educational administrators at the beginning of this chapter, the reader can find exciting, practical examples of designing a simple but technology-enhanced infrastructure in order to use emerging technologies as communication and collaborative tools, especially with students and their parents. Whereas Chapter 3 reinforces the need for effective professional development, this chapter focuses on a school district's cyber-infrastructure. Chapter 4 links the fourth NETP goal of educators' access to emerging technologies to the ISTE NETS.A standard of high expectations for administrators to use digital age tools in supporting their own professional practice of collaborating and communicating with key education stakeholders. Professional practice can only be improved if there is access to the school district's technology-enhanced infrastructure.

The School District's Cyber-Infrastructure

NETP Goal 4: "Infrastructure: Access and Enable" aims to improve student achievement by giving students and educators access to information, content creation, and online learning communities. The five categories of NETP Goal 4 are as follows:

4.0 Infrastructure: All students and educators will have access to a comprehensive infrastructure for learning when and where they need it. To meet this goal, we recommend the following actions:

4.1 Ensure students and educators have broadband access to the Internet and adequate wireless connectivity both in and out of school [. . .].

4.2 Ensure that every student and educator has at least one Internet access device and appropriate software and resources for research, communication, multimedia content creation, and collaboration for use in and out of school [. . .].

4.3 Support the development and use of open educational resources to promote innovative and creative opportunities for all learners and accelerate the development and adoption of new open technology-based learning tools and courses [. . .].

4.4 Build state and local education agency capacity for evolving an infrastructure for learning [. . .].

4.5 Develop and use interoperability standards for content and student-learning data to enable collecting and sharing resources and collecting, sharing, and analyzing data to improve decision making at all levels of our educational system [. . .].

4.6 Develop and use interoperability standards for financial data to enable data-driven decision making, productivity advances, and continuous improvement at all levels of our education system [. . .].

(U.S. Department of Education, 2010, pp. 61–62)

As instructional leaders and strategic planners, educational administrators and technology coordinators can facilitate student learning and meet the fourth goal of the National Education Technology Plan by utilizing the low-cost E-Rate discounts of the National Broadband Plan; by making Internet access devices available to every student and every teacher; by using open educational resources (OERs); and by effectively implementing cloud computing in their schools and districts. The school business administrator also plays a key role in ensuring that the district's technology infrastructure is both funded and efficient.

Four New Technology Trends

Four recent technology initiatives and trends are conducive to achieving the full integration of technology in learning because they improve the cyber-infrastructure of schools: the National Broadband Plan and its effects on E-Rate discounts; the proliferation of Internet access devices; the availability of OERs; and next-generation computing, often referred to as cloud computing.

The Federal Communications Commission (FCC) issued the National Broadband Plan (NETP Goal 4.1) in 2010 to provide a framework for connecting all homes and schools in the United States to high-speed Internet access. This new plan also simplified the application process and increased the $2.25 billion E-Rate funding by $950 million (Herbert, 2010) in order to offset the costs of public libraries and school districts connecting to broadband. As a result, more students and teachers have greater access to the Internet for learning and instructional opportunities: "The plan calls for expanded access to educational digital content, increased recognition of credits earned through online learning, refinements of digital data and interoperability standards, digital literacy promotion, and research and development of new broadband-enabled online learning systems" (U.S. Department of Education, 2010, p53). School district business administrators and superintendents should be aware of the E-Rate changes that encourage districts to adopt electronic learning records and to improve the transparency of presenting financial data. School districts can receive 20% to 90% E-Rate discounts on network connections, Internet access, and telecommunications services. The percentage of discount is calculated based on the number of students in a district who are eligible for the National School Lunch Program. In addition, the new E-Rate policies allow for funding of "wireless connectivity to portable learning devices," with anytime, anywhere opportunities for students to engage in multimedia educational activities. The National Broadband Plan's recognition of the value of online learning environments is also important for principals and superintendents to consider when dealing with credit recovery, advanced placement, and other virtual or cyber modes of delivering course content (Brooks-Young, 2006; Tadeja, 2010; Garland, 2011). Chapter 2 addresses the impact of a cyber-infrastructure upon learning in more detail.

The rapid proliferation of Internet access devices in students' personal use cannot be denied (Garland, 2006; Tadeja, 2011a), and the need for using these wireless platforms in education is recognized by the National Education Technology Plan Goal 4.2. The new cyber-infrastructure promotes the use of Internet access devices for 24/7 learning opportunities (Papa, 2010). According to the technology plan, Internet access devices can include "desktop computers, laptops, netbooks, public access kiosks, mobile phones, portable digital players, and wireless readers" (U.S. Department of Education, 2010, p54). One challenge is funding these access devices for students and teachers, while ensuring Internet safety and student privacy (Garland, 2006; Herbert, 2010); these issues are explored further in Chapter 6.

Open education resources are generally considered to be public domain teaching, learning, and educational resources. OERs can also be freely available over the Internet because of intellectual property licenses that permit the sharing of such resources for both educational and commercial purposes. National Education Technology Plan Goal 4.3 recognizes OERs as essential to the future of both P-12 and higher education. In some school districts and in many universities, OERs take the form of podcasts, e-books, digital libraries, and online courses. According to Schrum and Levin (2009, p94): "These sites provide free, open source software that can be hosted on your school or district server to provide blogs, discussion forums, collaborative authoring environments, peer-to-peer networking, newsletters, podcasts, picture galleries, file uploads, and downloads [. . .] creating and even replacing textbooks with content and curriculum found on the Internet by using widely available, free Web 2.0 tools and reusable learning objects, this is a very real possibility for many subjects, and it's a cost-saving measure, too." Thus, OER materials are only available online and have engaged the global learning community. As schools begin the 21st-century transition to more digital resources, such as changing from expensive hard copy-textbooks to more cost-effective e-books or OER "open textbooks," learners will have substantially more opportunities for learning and educators will have greater access to content (Tadeja, 2010, 2011a).

Is your school district facing budget cuts? School business administrators, principals, teachers, and superintendents would be wise to consider cost-effective E-Rate discounts, Internet access devices, and OERs as ways of improving student learning. In order to facilitate these changes, the school leader must build local education agency capacity for a digital age infrastructure (NETP Goal 4.4). By this, the NETP authors mean that in house data repositories should be replaced by less expensive and more secure cloud-based data centers for better capacity and privacy. Administrators are urged to implement this next generation of technology systems by reducing the number of servers and purchasing Software as a Service (SaaS) and Web applications from cloud-based data centers. According to Waters (2011, p. 30): "Leveraging a cloud-based service to house data off-site instead of maintaining your own data storage can enhance efficiencies, add flexibility, strengthen security, and cut costs by way of reduced person hours, personnel, and hardware investments." Cloudware can be a powerful collaborative tool because the same web-based resources are available 24/7 to authorized users in and out of the brick-and-mortar school buildings. Access to the data is programmable in cloud computing, which makes it easier to search and share. There can also be on-site private clouds, as well as off-site, backup, and/or public clouds. Cloud computing thus supports both academic and administrative functions for P-12 education.

Interoperability Standards

The district cyber-infrastructure should have "interoperability standards" for both curriculum content and student learning (NETP Goal 4.5). Although large and small school districts collect a great deal of data on students, there is a general lack of standardization and access to that information. New software and "data warehouses," modeled on data management systems used in business, can standardize data across all levels of school district operations. However, automated student records can be costly: "This is going to be a large, expensive project that can take anywhere from three to six months to prepare to implement once you have selected a vendor" (Brooks-Young, 2009, p. 162). For the budget-conscious school district, it is therefore recommended that pilot programs or incremental implementation be used in transitioning from one record-keeping system to another. If a school district already contracts with a software vendor for customized data storage, then the issue of transitioning from an older system to a newer, more effective one should be easily addressed with that existing contact, and cost-effective measures would be more likely to be negotiated. Incremental implementation could also mean keeping two record-keeping systems in place temporarily, such as one in-house and one warehoused on the cloud, until the transition is fully successful.

The authors of NETP Goal 4.6 encourage school districts to standardize financial data for increased productivity and school improvement. Effective data-based decision-making "is the process of compiling, reviewing, sharing, and using data to assist in improving schools, and, particularly, enhancing student achievement" (Kowalski et al., 2008, p. 103). Financial data in school districts generally includes budgets, purchase orders, facility records and maintenance, building projects, transportation and fuel, food services, inventories, and other accounts. School leaders should also ensure that they have technology-powered management information systems (MIS) to input, access, and organize all school district data according to state guidelines. States have different financial reporting criteria and data management systems, such as the Education Management Information System (EMIS), Ohio's statewide data collection system for all of its primary and secondary public schools. The EMIS reports include demographic, attendance, curriculum, financial data and test results (see http://www.ode.state.oh.us/GD/Templates/Pages/ODE). Data management systems can also be expanded to individualize student schedules. One example of this is the ASAP Class Management system, which assists school districts and other organizations in using one web-based portal in administering their course schedules (http://asapconnected.com/class-management-software.html).

Professional Practice in the Digital Age

The third NETS.A standard is focused on how administrators, program directors, and technology coordinators can support teachers and themselves in using the most effective digital age tools. There are four areas of ISTE NETS.A Standard 3 "Excellence in Professional Practice":

> Educational Administrators promote an environment of professional learning and innovation that empowers educators to enhance student learning through the infusion of contemporary technologies and digital resources. Educational Administrators:
>
> (a) allocate time, resources, and access to ensure ongoing professional growth in technology fluency and integration;
>
> (b) facilitate and participate in learning communities that stimulate, nurture, and support administrators, faculty, and staff in the study and use of technology;
>
> (c) promote and model effective communication and collaboration among stakeholders using digital-age tools;
>
> (d) stay abreast of educational research and emerging trends regarding effective use of technology and encourage evaluation of new technologies for their potential to improve student learning.
>
> (ISTE, 2009, p. 11)

Empowering teachers to make changes in their instructional practice is a powerful means to help them meet their students' needs (NETS.A Standard 3). The results of a study by Bogler (2005) showed that teachers who perceived that they could make positive changes in their instructional methods were most likely to also improve their commitment to professional development. Whereas the previous chapter examines what constitutes effective professional development methods, the focus here is how an effective cyber-infrastructure and the use of emerging technologies are linked to successful digital age in-service and communication activities for teachers and administrators alike.

Technology Integration in Practice

Do educational administrators face technology challenges similar to those faced by teachers in their own use of the cyber-infrastructure to improve student learning? Administrators and teacher leaders should take personal responsibility for understanding changes in technology integration in their buildings and classrooms, rather than simply relying on technology support staff. Despite the ongoing development of new technologies, it is up to the building-level staff, district personnel, and educational leaders to move schools into the digital age (Larson et al., 2010). For instance, in the leader reflection piece at the beginning of this chapter, one can read about how a superintendent and principal in the same New Hampshire school district learned, designed, and implemented an enhanced cyber-infrastructure in order to more fully communicate and collaborate with administrators, teachers, and parents for improved student learning.

Continuous in-service training, possible only with the proper allocation of time and resources, is an important element in integrating technology at any school site (NETS.A Standard 3.a). Undoubtedly, there are kindergarteners now entering schools armed with computer literacy skills and who are socially "tech savvy." Teachers sometimes find that they are unable to cope with curricular technology goals in addition to dealing with the demanding instructional strategies of a standards-based curriculum. One way to meet this challenge is for school principals and technology coordinators to continuously offer training to teachers so that they master even the most basic technology skills, such as the effective use of blogs, discussion boards, and educational websites. In Gulbahar's study (2007), teachers were found to prefer active and applied learning, as well as one-to-one tutorials, as the best methods for in-service training. A more substantive discussion of effective professional development is provided in Chapter 3. By building a digital age infrastructure, principals and technology coordinators provide access to additional instructional materials and technology tools for all stakeholders in the educational process.

Do you have Professional Learning Communities (PLCs) in your school or district? PLCs, also discussed in the previous two chapters, are natural collaborative forums for administrators and teachers alike to study and implement emerging technologies (NETS.A Standard 3.b). Lieberman and Mace (2009) describe how accomplished practices can be shared between classrooms and between practitioners with varying levels of experience. One simple example stems from networked computers and printers. An individual can easily share information and print out documents remotely from the convenience of his or her home, a local coffee shop, or another remote site. Another common trend is for homeowners, when away from home and perhaps on their smartphones, to use networked cameras to watch their pets or properties. These same digital tools apply to networked learning communities, in which valuable and rich resources from individuals who carry expertise are shared. No longer are there individual experts, but rather there is a pool of professionals and collaborators who can create ideas, engage the students, and facilitate improved learning (Jonassen et al., 1998).

Many educators can benefit from a networked learning community that links other professionals regionally and globally to the education platform. An education technology idea from London will no longer be limited to the regional concentration of that area, but can spread to local learning communities across the globe. Students in Omaha, Nebraska, for instance, can see and experience the same idea as those students in England. Electronic communication tools, such as email, bulletin boards, virtual networks, and blogs, can serve to stitch knowledge and meaning together, especially in today's fast-paced 21st-century learning communities.

Communication Tools for Administrators and Teachers

Another digital age tool to enhance PLCs and communication is the blog. The use of blogging by teachers and students was briefly reviewed in Chapter 2. It has also become a popular phenomenon among educational leaders. However, some school administrators have caught on to the idea of indiscriminately jotting down their thoughts for the whole world to see online. Although this provides parents and the community with a glimpse of what may be happening in the school, this technique is short sighted. Administrators should focus instead on opportunities to discuss how educational technology is helping them to reach their school district's goals and learning objectives. Blogging is done effectively when there is a commitment and a discipline to making frequent entries. The use of Twitter to get information instantaneously is seen as critical for some individuals; but blogging takes on a greater purpose. It requires the time and energy to express one's thoughts on educational issues and it serves an additional purpose by inviting other stakeholders to respond to those ideas. Listening and self-reflection, therefore, become distinctive pieces of successful blogging. Some sites require more technical "know-how" to navigate a successful blog, while others provide a more seamless experience. Other elements to consider with advanced blogging include using video, screen casting, podcasting, and integrating outside videos from the web. Few sites are now reminiscent of the days when blogging was simply a tool for writing down your thoughts. An administrator can easily enhance his or her blog presentation with the use of various new multimedia.

A school district in Saugus, California, has recently utilized ELGG, an open source social networking application, to devise a unique way to create two blogging communities: one created for the students and the other for the teachers, staff, and community. The latter allows individuals to suggest websites, share handouts, generate ideas, or begin a discussion of complex concepts. It also acts as a repository of information that would benefit the teacher and the students whom they serve. The community for students is designed much in the same way, but utilizes avatars to protect students' identity. All of this is done under protected software to constantly monitor comments and inappropriate behavior. But the power behind this collaborative effort is notable since this is now using open source technology to harness the need to share with one another.

Technology coordinators across the country have spoken to the authors at length about moving away from an aging top-down approach to using classroom technologies that embrace what is now called a personal learning environment. Users who surf the Internet for information usually do it by searching through multiple sites or mashed up spaces such as blog posts and news feeds. Students are doing this more and more, as well as looking for resources that can help them search for information. Administrators need to find ways to utilize these resources and offer them to both teachers and students. The ELGG community is one way to do this; but there are other sites as well that provide information, including Ning, del.icio.us, and Grouply.

Twitters and blogs are also effective mediums that can be used by educational leaders to communicate to the public. A school district near Erie, Pennsylvania, has used blogs to build a school alumni website, while another school in South Yorkshire, England, has been using blog sites as a repository for student electronic portfolios. A student will accumulate projects throughout his or her school years and house them on a district server. The student organizes the work in corresponding files to make it easier for teachers to access and assess the work. When the student graduates or is ready for a job, he or she has access to the files to use or transfer them to his or her own server. This has worked well for years in this small community. Of more importance, it has allowed the district to use technology in order to connect with the students in the real world.

But blogging is not the only tool that one should consider when promoting the effective use of technology. Sites such as polleverywhere.com and polldaddy.com are a means to get real-time responses. A principal, for instance, can use his or her blog to communicate the results of student academic learning or engagement in school activities. In one school community near Tucson, Arizona, students were given the opportunity to use their cell phones to generate ideas for an upcoming school event. Using Poll Everywhere, students gathered after school in the main "quad" on campus and were allowed to cast their votes by texting (only once) to a specified number. Results from the votes cast were immediately shown on a screen. Because the votes were informal and the texting was only done to generate ideas, students were given the chance to integrate their own technology tools with something related to their school. A more formal vote on the same event was later cast using traditional voting methods in order to meet the needs of those who did not have access to a cell phone. But administrators were applauded by their community counterparts and parents for allowing students to utilize their cell phones, albeit informally, to integrate technology and school-related business. Since then, this school district and many like it across the country have changed their acceptable use policies (AUPs) to include the use of cell phones as a direct result of adopting the educational benefits of Poll Everywhere.

In another example, high school students in a peer counseling class near Casper, Wyoming, use Poll Everywhere on a weekly basis during their group discussions. The teacher poses a question to the students in which they can use Poll Everywhere to respond. Because the question is sometimes sensitive and because teenagers can become anxious about sharing how they really feel, Poll Everywhere is used to encourage honest responses since respondents can remain anonymous. At the same time, students conduct real-time collaborative assessments with their peers. Students are now bringing in their tablets, iPads, and cell phones to engage in this weekly polling in this Wyoming high school.

Educators from around the country and around the world are trying to find ways to harness the power of social media websites such as Facebook. Edmodo is one means of providing a safe and secure social learning network. The site allows teachers to post websites, provide feedback, and generate links to help their students understand content. The authors have spoken to educators across the United States and have discovered that many of them are using similar sites to engage and collaborate with their students.

Social Media Classroom and Classroom 2.0 are similar websites that use participative technologies such as blogs, comments, forums, social bookmarking, and video commenting to deliver curriculum in real time. These digital communication tools also allow teachers to experiment and share with other educators from across the globe. The term "collaboratory" is often used to describe this phenomenon where groups of individuals, including businesses, teachers, and community, generate information about topics or ideas to teach each other. WeCollaborate is another social networking site for educators and students but primarily uses Blackboard to deliver information. There are others which support different platforms from learning, such as Library 2.0, Student 2.0, Teacher 2.0, Learn Central, Kid Blog, and Twiducate. Some of these networked learning communities are further described in Chapter 3 on professional development.

Technorati is a website dedicated to searching and promoting the use of blogs. There are literally thousands of blog sites; many are dedicated to the fields of technology, education, and learning. When all three of these concepts merge, collaboration takes place and the stimulation of creativity and innovation is nearly limitless. Online blogging is one way to promote both local and national learning communities. A blog is ever changing, as is the information it provides. An administrator's blog allows others to follow the leader's ideas, and it can provide helpful educational information derived online. Blogging becomes a collaborative adventure for educators and students alike, as it allows questions to be asked in the hopes that answers will be sought. For further assistance, readers should refer to some popular blogging websites at the end of this book. In the leaders' reflection section at the beginning of this chapter, the reader will also find ample examples of how a principal and a superintendent in one New Hampshire school district are using digital age collaboration tools, such as blogs, Twitter, wikis, and podcasts.

Technology for Collaboration

How does your school or district involve the parents and guardians in the learning of their children? The types of instructional collaborative activities of many school district PLCs can be extended to a wider audience (NETS.A Standard 3.c), such as parents and community members. For instance, classroom management systems such as PowerSchool and Zangle now feature and promote tools for teachers and principals to use in order to assist parents in better understanding how their children are performing. The newer grade and student behavior management programs help parents and guardians to connect with their children's grades, behavioral issues, and school notices about upcoming events. Thus, these technology management tools enable not only teachers but also principals to connect with parents about student issues. One caveat is that not all parents or guardians will have access to these digital age technology tools, so the educator must ensure that there are additional ways of communicating with school community stakeholders who might be "digitally excluded."

SchoolFusion is an online learning community that has devised a broader platform of collaboration tools and community management tools. A superintendent could utilize this service that specifically targets the K-12 environment. Teachers and students benefit with the use of their paperless technology to engage students in numerous multimedia aspects. But SchoolFusion is just one of many collaboration tools in which the approach is based on improving student learning. The results of a study by Heaton-Shrestha and colleagues (2009) suggest that both student engagement and performance in learning are increased when social networking tools are integrated in instructional practice.

For superintendents and the executive cabinet members, it may be necessary to establish a process in which stakeholders can communicate with them on an ongoing basis. Utilizing as many collaboration technology and contemporary communication tools as possible can help the larger community to feel as though they are connected to this district-level group. It can also help to organize the many streams of requests that come from administrators, union representatives, teachers, parents, students, and the community at large. Economides (2008) discusses the use of "culture-aware collaborative learning" in order to better understand and collaborate with the culture in which we work. It is not enough that we simply listen to the needs of our stakeholders. The No Child Left Behind Act and more recent federal initiatives have asked educators to pay attention to the diverse needs of various cultures within our learning community.

Educational leaders must be sensitive to the cultural needs of the community they serve. One way to do this is to develop synchronous real-time platforms. We are now depending upon computers to be used much in the same way we communicate with each other, in real time in both audio and video interaction. This means that we are no longer interested in simple chatting but are interested in integrating video as well. The way in which we communicate today is vastly different from the almost linear and two-way communication tools of yesterday. Today we utilize different tools to help our audience understand us better. Facebook and Twitter have drastically altered the way in which we interact with family and friends. Other networking sites, such as LinkedIn and Google Plus, enhance our professional roles. These are tools to create seamless and natural ways for us to communicate with other stakeholders in the educational process. Superintendents and administrators can do this, too. Teachers are also not limited to the virtual classroom of yesteryear. Rather, students, teachers, and administrators can all now become engaged in developing virtual platforms (Demski, 2010).

Blackboard Collaborate (formerly Elluminate and Wimba Classroom), WebEx, and Adobe Connect are all examples of creating synchronous real-time platforms. These are sometimes referred to as "live meetings" or virtual venues for collaborative meetings. Using any of these systems produces an experience that allows people to see and interact with one another, discuss points, debate, draw virtual diagrams, and chat in real time. To imagine what something like these digital age tools could do for administrators and teachers who work with their community members, the reader has only to read the leader reflection piece at the beginning of this chapter.

Blackboard Collaborate, along with other real-time synchronous environments, houses tools within its site so that individuals can host real-time meetings. In several of the schools the authors have visited, teachers were in front of a webcam at their home or offices and speaking to students from across the country to discuss ideas on assignments, to share questions, or to collaborate on projects. But the authors also found other ways to conduct these "live meetings." Technology studios should be considered when building the cyber-infrastructure of the school and district. There are numerous schools across the United States and abroad that have technology plans in place to create and develop technology studios that combine elements of video production and a multimedia stage. California State University Polytechnic, Pomona, for instance, houses a technology studio, named Studio 6. Here instructors can "amp up" their PowerPoint presentations by including themselves within it. The studio has the capability to "green screen" individuals into their PowerPoints so that they appear to be standing in front of each slide. Administrators can emulate the same thing without having to purchase the expensive equipment to house a technology studio. UStream is a real-time lifecasting service that can videotape anyone using a simple webcam. A school administrator can sit behind his or her desk and describe some of the policies or school news in real time while the staff, students, and even parents watch from the comforts of their home, or in a school lab, or through the use of a projector and a teacher computer console. Students can do the same thing by creating a broadcast of the latest information of their school. Superintendents and technology coordinators can discuss issues related to the global perspective. This kind of lifecasting can also be archived, like a book, to be seen later for years to come.

Sliderocket.com is another presentation tool similar to Microsoft PowerPoint software. But a closer look at Sliderocket reveals a slightly different approach to the presentation tools of today. Sliderocket allows users to utilize and bring in real-time tweets, link Facebook accounts, collaborate with other users, and add comments all within the presentation. A tool like this could enable administrators to share ideas and solicit real-time comments from individuals who share the presentation. The implications are profound for teachers and students in the classroom since children do not always think in linear platforms. In fact, looking at students and how they communicate using social media sites suggests that they solicit acceptance with certain things they do or places they go. Why can't a presentation tool do the same thing? Aren't we doing the same thing when we come together in a conference room to meet? Don't we ask each other about our thoughts and don't we try to connect with these thoughts through as many outlets as possible? Problem solving in the 21st century means that individuals bring in as much information as they can to find real solutions (Roe, 2011).

The school librarian or media specialist is another stakeholder who can be utilized to collaborate in the use of digital age tools to improve student learning. Librarians are responsible for promoting literacy and the love of reading. But many schools are also providing librarians and media specialists with professional development for integrating technology in the classroom, sharing information about new resources, and demonstrating innovative instructional tools (Dees, et al., 2010). According to the American Association of School Librarians (AASL), librarians are now media specialists who implement standards for the 21st-century learner with a Lesson Plan Database, an interactive, collaborative tool for teaching essential learning skills (http://www.ala.org/aasl/guidelinesandstandards/guidelinesandstandards). As media specialists, school librarians also compile collections of websites or databases for educators and learners.

Technology Teacher Certification

The last section of NETS.A Standard 3 is focused on the need for school administrators to be skilled in the research, implementation, and evaluation of emerging technologies. Some experts in these areas are completing certification programs for technology coordinators and technology teachers.

Today's teachers are scrambling to catch up with the "GenX," "Gen-Y," and "Gen-Z" students, who arrive in schools as "tech savvy" "digital natives." Social networking tools are not yet fully integrated within effective instructional practices in public schools (Garland, 2011). In addition to the technology coordinator, a recently certified technology teacher can help to implement and support the technology infrastructure properly, both for the "digital native" students or new teachers and administrators, as well for as the "digital immigrant" veteran teachers or administrators. Unfortunately, state-level certification credentials for a school district-level instructional technology leader are limited to only a few states. Educational leaders are encouraged to be state-level policy-makers in order to achieve the goal of school district technology coordinator certification in all states.

Technology Resources for Administrators

It is important for principals, program directors, superintendents, and technology coordinators to subscribe to journals and other professional publications that can help them to keep up to date on the latest research on the use of technology to improve student learning. School districts and their respective libraries or media centers need to subscribe to databases so both they and their students have access to electronic publications that offer the latest in how technology is integrated in schools, districts, and even statewide initiatives. More time and energy should be focused on how to prepare students for learning beyond the secondary level. Placing more value on these kinds of digital age resources allows students to get a jump-start on new research. What is learned and "hot" today in technology may not necessarily be "hot" a month or a year from now. Continual access to new research, available in databases such as EBSCO or ERIC or LexisNexis, meets these challenges and can provide a better understanding of where the world of technology is going. The companion website for this text offers many helpful resources on accessing information on the latest technology trends in education.

TIPS FOR SCHOOL LEADERS

1 In order to enable a technology-enhanced school district infrastructure, give easy but appropriate access to data for students, educators, and parents/guardians.

2 Communicate with your district's parents and community members through digital age tools such as podcasts, Twitter accounts, email listservs, wiki websites, screencasts, or automatic call systems.

3 Use cloudware such as Google documents to develop and share policies, technology plans, or project work.

4 Increase the efficiency of your district's operations with web-based applications for tracking and revising purchase orders, federal and state grants, and other financial reports.

5 Use data-based decision-making to improve student achievement through technologies that will assist you in disaggregating data on the state test, in differentiating instruction according to individual scores on tests, and in giving teachers data for planning intervention strategies while instruction occurs.

6 Be aware of the E-Rate changes that encourage districts to adopt electronic learning records, to improve financial data transparency, and to fund wireless connectivity to portable devices for students.

7 Improve your operational efficiency and security by reducing the number of servers and purchasing Software as a Service (SaaS) and Web applications from cloud-based data centers.

8 Implement a technology-powered management information system (MIS) to input, access, and organize school district financial data.

9 Communicate with parents through newer grade and student behavior management programs in order for them to access their children's grades, behavioral issues, and school notices about upcoming events.

10 Keep updated on the latest educational technology research through district-level subscriptions to statewide and national databases.

Summary

This chapter provides educational leaders with practical suggestions on how to achieve NETP Goal 4 on access to emerging technologies as well as NETS.A Standard 3 on urging school administrators to use digital age tools to improve their own professional practice of collaborating and communicating with other educators and community members. The leader reflection at the beginning of this chapter gives practical ideas on how a superintendent and a principal in the same school district developed an enhanced cyber-infrastructure, which resulted in better communication and collaboration with not only other administrators and teachers, but with students, parents, and other community members. However, as much of this chapter indicates, updating the school district's technology infrastructure does not have to be expensive because of the use of cloud-based document storage, existing websites, open educational resources, free Web 2.0 tools, and E-rate discounts. Once the technology-enhanced infrastructure is in place, the educational leader can more easily engage in adapting the district to the digital age. In Chapter 5, the administrator will learn how to become a transformational leader with the recruitment of "tech savvy" educators and the establishment of strategic technology partnerships within the district itself and with other organizations. The ultimate goal of improved student performance is thus best served by educators' effective use of emerging communication and collaboration technology tools.

School administrators who rate themselves and their schools or districts with scores of 5 and 4 are already meeting the standards indicated in those items. Ratings of 1 or 2 would indicate areas of needed professional growth by either the school district, or the school leader, or both in order to meet the NETS.A standards or NETP goals.

TABLE 4.1 School Administrator's Technology Leadership Self-Assessment Survey: The Technology Infrastructure (Chapter 4)

Directions: Please respond to each item by circling a number from 1 to 5, where 5 = strongly agree; 4 = agree; 3 = neutral; 2 = disagree; 1 = strongly disagree.

This survey is based on National Education Technology Plan (NETP) Goal 4 (NETP 4.1 to 4.6) and National Educational Technology Standards and Performance Indicators for Administrators (NETS.A) Standard 3 (NETS.A 3.a, 3.b, 3.c, 3.d, 3.e).

5 = strongly agree (SA); 4 = agree (A); 3 = neutral (N); 2 = disagree (D); 1 = strongly disagree (SD)	SA	A	N	D	SD
1 All of our students and teachers have wireless broadband Internet connectivity (NETP 4.1):					
(a) in school buildings;	5	4	3	2	1
(b) outside of school buildings and at home.	5	4	3	2	1
2 All of our students and teachers have Internet access devices with updated software for multimedia content creation, research, communication, and collaboration (NETP 4.2):					
(a) in school buildings;	5	4	3	2	1
(b) outside of school buildings and at home.	5	4	3	2	1
3 Our school or district fully utilizes open educational resources (OERs) as technology tools (NETP 4.3).	5	4	3	2	1
4 Administrators build local education capacity for technology infrastructure (NETP 4.4).	5	4	3	2	1
5 The district has interoperability technologies for student data-based decisions (NETP 4.5).	5	4	3	2	1
6 The district has interoperability technologies for financial data-based decisions (NETP 4.6).	5	4	3	2	1
7 The district allocates adequate time and resources to professional development in technology integration (NETS.A 3.a).	5	4	3	2	1
8 Our district encourages Professional Learning Communities (PLCs) for administrators and teachers to study and use technology (NETS.A 3.b).	5	4	3	2	1
9 Our district uses digital age tools in communicating and collaborating with these education stakeholders (NETS.A 3.c):					
(a) students;	5	4	3	2	1
(b) teachers;	5	4	3	2	1
(c) principals;	5	4	3	2	1
(d) program directors;	5	4	3	2	1
(e) superintendents	5	4	3	2	1
(f) Board of Education members;	5	4	3	2	1

5 = strongly agree (SA); 4 = agree (A); 3 = neutral (N); 2 = disagree (D); 1 = strongly disagree (SD)	SA	A	N	D	SD
(g) parents;	5	4	3	2	1
(h) taxpayers and community members.	5	4	3	2	1
10 As an educational leader, I study and evaluate how emerging technologies can be used to improve student learning (NETS.A 3.d).	5	4	3	2	1

V. E. Garland and C. Tadeja, 2012

DISCUSSION QUESTIONS

1 In what ways can you develop networked learning communities in your own school or district? How might you draw from various experts? Create a graphic visual to describe what this process would look like and share it with a group or a partner.

2 Real-time collaboration is an essential key to facilitate learning and to propel the uses of today's modern technology. How can pre-service and in-service administrators develop real-time collaborative activities? What would these look like in your own professional learning communities?

3 How can the sharing of student-learning data be improved in your school or district? Discuss the accessibility of assessment information to various stakeholders in the education process, such as teachers, parents, students, and administrators.

4 Does your school or district ensure that all teachers and students have at least one Internet access device? If not, how can the obstacles to "one computer per student" be overcome?

5 In the leader reflection for Chapter 4, a New Hampshire superintendent and his elementary principal discuss their widespread use of emerging technologies for communication, collaboration, operations, and data-based decision-making. How do these two administrators link their district's cyber-infrastructure to improved instructional practices? Compare the effectiveness of the digital tools used in the Hopkinton School District, New Hampshire, with those used in your school or district.

6 Based on your responses to the self-assessment for Chapter 4, what are the next steps you might take in improving the technology infrastructure in your school or district? What technology resources would you need in your own professional e-portfolio in order to assist you in achieving your goals?

5
Systemic Change with Personnel and Partnerships in Technology

Synopsis

Since information and communication technologies (ICTs) are increasing exponentially each month in the business and social sectors, it is incumbent upon school administrators to carefully examine these innovations in order to plan and implement systemic change in their school districts. The previous chapter provided suggestions on how school leaders can significantly improve the technology infrastructure of their school districts in order to enhance communication and collaboration with educators and community members. Chapter 5 explains how school administrators can use new digital learning resources effectively in order to lead organizational changes which meet their district's learning goals. The two key elements to successful systemic improvement of the educational organization are professional personnel and educational partnerships. Both stakeholder groups must be highly trained, effective implementers of technology tools. Principals and district-level leaders must lead efforts in systemic change that will improve student learning in their schools. The following two leader reflections are examples of best practice in leading schools of the future with digital age technologies. Throughout the chapter, current research and practical applications for school leaders are aligned with NETS.A Standard 4 on systemic improvement.

Reflections of a Chief Technology Officer in Kansas

New uses for technology continue to have significant impacts on the world we live in. It has changed and enhanced how we communicate with others, purchase goods and services, become entertained, and it has opened up a world of knowledge to be available at our fingertips. The rate of technology integration into our lives continues to accelerate at an ever increasing rate.

We have experienced a number of innovative uses of technology in the classroom over the years, from the use of interactive systems and collaboration technologies to enabling anywhere learning through the use of mobile technologies. The majority of these education technology innovations are augments and substitutes for the traditional instruction that occurs in our classrooms. Based [on] the definitions that Dr. Ruben Puentedura developed, we are working towards the next stage of innovation for our schools by redefining instruction and enhancing our ability to personalize learning and make effective educational decisions through the use of information and data.

There are three core ideas our district views with utmost importance in regard to the use of technology and our resources, and are the essence of our technology plans:

1   the *inspiration* to provide personalized student learning, also the heart and soul of the district's strategic plan, to help every student attain and put into daily practice the skills necessary to move beyond the basics of digital-age learning;

2   the *imagination* to accurately envision a future that includes new and unique uses for current technology, or the use of technology unknown to us at this moment;

3   the *innovation* to understand that we cannot possibly teach our students how to use all technology that may exist in the future, and they will be better served if we provide them with foundational skills that build self-confidence, thus enabling them to explore and discover new ways to learn using technology.

These core ideas will help us answer the call of our strategic plan, to make sure our students are college or career ready and that they have a firm grasp of technology to be effective in the 21st century.

It will be the three core principles embedded in our strategic technology planning and strong partnerships throughout the district that will allow us all to collectively move forward with a deeper level of technology integration in our district. All levels of staff from district administration, building administration, and teachers are needed to buy into the core principles and the technology strategic direction of the school district for technology integration. These partnerships will allow us to take policy to practice and create an innovative environment for our students to learn in.

Our primary strategic focus as a district is to provide an "Education beyond Expectations" experience through personalized learning for our students. We began to look at ways that data-driven decision-making could assist us in providing personalized learning opportunities. Four years ago we started the journey of leveraging the data contained in all of our separate systems in a unified way. We began by aggregating all of the data from our various systems, about our students and their learning, into a data warehouse. By having this data in a single location, it has allowed us to identify trends and correlations in student information that were not readily apparent before then. This has enabled us to make more informed decisions around instructional supports and curriculum decisions than we have been able to in the past. We continue to look for additional opportunities to leverage this data to assist us in making better decisions and personalize learning opportunities for our students so they can continue to have an "Education beyond Expectations" experience.

One of our other primary goals is to prepare our students to live and work in the 21st century, to be a "digital citizen." "Digital citizenship" may sound like a very technical term; but the definition simply details the ways that responsible citizens can transfer that mastery to the world of technology. It goes beyond the concept of possessing inherent skills as "digital natives" to a point of our students purposefully developing an overall technology fluency. Our students will demonstrate this fluency through learning and using sound ethical judgments and practices in the digital world; understanding the new technologies that are available to them and applying them in daily use; and the active use of these new technologies to continually support and expand their current learning opportunities.

Our vision for our teachers and their use of technology will come to fruition when we can say that our learning spaces are places where our teachers do not hesitate to incorporate state-of-the-art technology into their lesson plans not only because it is available, but because they have been exposed to professional learning opportunities that enable them to successfully integrate the technology into their instruction. In addition, this vision extends to our school administrators. We equip our administrators with mobile technology tools to enable them to stay connected throughout their building and have real-time access to data and student information. This mobile connectivity allows them to conduct informal walk-throughs, and to stay in touch with staff instructional practices and provide just-in-time feedback to the teachers.

We expect our administrators in our schools to model the use of technology to our teachers. Through the use of technology, professional development supports, and technology use modeling by our administrators, our teachers will find many new ways to innovate, and through this innovation, they will be able to teach our students in a personalized way that engages and motivates them.

Greg DeYoung is the executive director for information technology and the chief information officer for the Blue Valley School District in Overland Park, Kansas. Prior to working at Blue Valley, Greg was the director of campus technology for Eastern Illinois University, and assistant director for information technology at the University of Illinois. Greg has over 20 years of extensive experience in information technology and now works in one of the largest school districts in Kansas, covering 34 schools serving a total population of 22,500 students, including 5 award-winning high schools.

Reflections of an Online Education Coordinator in Georgia

Technology has changed the way people live and work. At work, technology is embraced as a mechanism for increasing profits and staying competitive. At home, technology is embraced for entertainment, security, and daily chores. At school, however, technology often remains a fringe element outside the mainstream of teaching and learning. Consequently, a school administrator who wishes to effectively implement technology as a transformational change will understand the dual nature of technology and will encourage both teachers and students to use their personal technology at school.

In Forsyth County Schools, Georgia, school principals can choose whether or not they want to provide Internet connectivity for personal devices on their campus. Initially, five principals felt a Bring Your Own Technology (BYOT) program was worth the risks and allowed students to bring personal devices to school. These principals supported their teachers by understanding there would be a learning curve and that mistakes were bound to occur. In addition, they allowed time for teachers to assimilate greater student collaboration and project-based learning into their lessons. The principals were rewarded with greater student engagement and with less discipline issues concerning the technology (since personal devices were no longer contraband). Although it has been only a year into the implementation, we now have over 20 schools doing BYOT and we are conducting site visits for school districts across the nation and Canada who wish to see first hand the benefits BYOT can bring in our own district.

In today's workplace, blue-collar jobs require mastery of proprietary technology. Automotive mechanics use computer analytical equipment to diagnose engine and transmission problems. Truck drivers use GPS technology to map out the most efficient delivery route. Subcontractors use project management software to ensure that the construction of a building stays on schedule. In fact, it is a cliché to say teaching is the only profession that has not drastically been transformed by technology.

The technology being used in these non-white-collar jobs is not the office desktop computer running productivity software. This technology is often composed of GPS units, electronic probes/sensors, and other hand-held devices designed to do a specific job. Cell phones and various other communication devices could be added to the list. Such technology bears a closer resemblance to the electronic gaming devices used by students for entertainment and leisure than they do to the desktop computer. Yet, for the most part, schools provide very little opportunities for students to learn this type of technology.

We have provided PASCO electronic probes/sensors and digital microscopes in our science labs. We provided a set of GPS units to each secondary school. Also, each classroom has an interactive white board and a document camera. Except for isolated instances where outstanding teachers went beyond what was expected, the use of these devices is directly proportional to the supervision of the building principal. Administrators who take the time and effort to make classroom visits to see technology-enhanced lessons have more technology-enhanced lessons in their schools. Dr. Gary Davidson of Lambert High School is one such principal. He uses an "app" on his iPhone to record his classroom visits, and emails the teacher with his observation as he is leaving the classroom.

Technology has also changed our personal and family life. We send birthday cards online, map the route for the family vacation online, and order pizza online. The traditional arbiters of all friendly disputes – Hoyle, Webster, and the Britannica Encyclopedia – are consulted online. We preview a film's trailer online, read the movie critic reviews online, and then buy the movie tickets online. To our students, the devices that we call "technology" are merely common household appliances.

Students are embedded in home technology (handheld devices, gaming consoles, and cell phones); but school technology is not the same. Although schools exist in a nebulous area between work and home, schools have implemented technology using, almost exclusively, the enterprise model taken from the corporate world (locked-down desktops, restricted network, and standardization of equipment). Perhaps the resistance that many teachers have towards instructional technology stems from an inherent discomfort with such a "corporate" approach. The thoughtful school administrators should look at home technology and convince their IT [information technology] department to kill the enterprise in favor of BYOT and similar policies that support social networking and other Web 2.0 endeavors. To make an argument for the best constructivist environment as one in which personal technology is used, school administrators should comprehend the concept of "virtualization."

Depending upon context, the term "virtual" has various connotations. In using such terms as virtual school, virtual lab, virtual classroom, and virtual teacher, most educators are unaware that the word "virtual" doesn't mean "computerized," but rather refers to a process in which "software acts as hardware." The opposite of virtual is not "real," but physical. In other words, physical entities that exist in time or space are replaced by non-physical entities that display the salient qualities of the physical entities. This meaning of virtual is paramount in understanding the virtualization of school.

The virtualization of school is a two-part process of, first, abstracting the attributes and behaviors of an educational object (the physical entity) and removing those attributes and behaviors that are irrelevant; and, second, using technology to recreate the educational object in ways that drastically rethink space, time, and resources. Just as a computer scientist uses abstraction to understand and solve complicated problems by discarding the superfluous, educators can use abstraction to isolate and solve pedagogical problems by discarding issues of tardiness, lunchroom management, PA announcements, club day, pep rallies, fundraising, and a thousand other non-academic demands that prevent the traditional school from effectively educating children.

For the school administrators, the concept of virtualization is important; otherwise, any change using technology will only be of first-order magnitude. For example, the "read this chapter, do these questions, and if we have time we will have a class discussion" is not an instructional model worthy of duplication. But many online courses replicate this type of instruction, albeit in a digital form. School administrators must guide their teachers to using technology to "do that which cannot be done any other way" lest our digital projectors become expensive overhead projectors, our computers become very expensive typewriters, and our Learning Management System becomes a very expensive homework hotline.

Virtualization in education includes the following examples.

A traditional high school course is transformed into an online course:

- Retain the standards to be mastered by the student and the evidence needed to prove that those standards were mastered.

- Ignore class periods, schedule conflicts, the number of desks in the classroom, etc.

- Place course content onto the Internet so that anyone at any time and any place (with an Internet connection) can access the course content.

Group instruction into differentiated instruction:

- Retain the design qualities that address learning styles and that promote student engagement.

- Ignore the traditional presence of a face-to-face teacher.

- Use the adaptive release of content materials along with blogs, wikis, puzzles, games, podcasting, and other Web 2.0 tools to provide for differences in learning styles and interest levels.

School attendance becomes an expectation of student progress:

- Retain the expectation that all students can learn.

- Ignore specific seat-time requirements.

- Electronically track the amount of time that students are online and electronically monitor their progress through the prescribed curriculum.

In all three of the above examples, technology is the mechanism that allows the possibility of virtualization. The failure to abstract the salient qualities of an educational object during the virtualization process will lead to the mere electronic replication of the ineffective methodology of the past. As we move into the future, the proper virtualization of school will transform rigid classrooms into agile, differentiated instructional environments. In fact, as the traditional way of "doing school" is a result of 20th-century technology, the 21st century way of "doing school" will be a result of 21st-century technology.

School districts will benefit from virtualization through:

- better use of existing educational resources;

- lower cost of new educational resources;

- flexibility in developing and deploying new instructional environments;

- significantly smaller physical plants.

The school district of the future will need the flexibility to deploy educational services quickly and reliably, as student needs change. A Learning Management System (LMS) will provide a flexible pool of virtual courses that can be deployed across the district with relative ease. As virtual courses are deployed and moved around the district at will, management of the virtual infrastructure becomes a crucial factor in ensuring that the complexity of the infrastructure is minimized. Effective use of the LMS will also help school districts contain school building sprawl, thus reducing deployment and operation costs. Furthermore, the LMS is rapidly developing into an integrated educational operations management solution.

In Forsyth County, each teacher and student has access to the LMS. We average 8,000 students online at 7:00 pm every weeknight. We use the LMS for everything from student instruction, to professional learning, to bus driver training, to the NFHS Quilting Club. The Learning Object Repository is full of thousands of teacher-produced learning objects. Our LMS has allowed us to extend the school day, create more teacher collaboration, place a stronger focus on standards, and provide greater communications with all stakeholders.

With the use of a LMS, the virtualization of school can achieve results not otherwise possible. For example, career academics are often implemented as "schools within a school." Often this presents great logistical difficulties due to the limited resources in one school. However, virtualization can pool physical resources from several physical entities to form numerous virtual academies that can function as independent schools or programs. This same method can be used for other programs like advanced placement (AP) classes, credit recovery, etc. It can even be used for clubs, work programs, and other special interest groups that may not have enough students to justify supporting at a single school.

Forsyth County's NOBLE Endeavor was a proven way to implement the virtualization of school. In this approach, each high school schedules a content area teacher to the first period to facilitate the online instruction of his/her content specialization. School A could house the math teacher, school B, the English teacher, school C the social studies, and so on. Since teachers are facilitating rather than delivering content, many courses in a content area could be offered. The students would be physically assigned to a computer lab at their home school and would be monitored by the home school teacher while that teacher facilitated students across the district in his/her particular content area. Students who proved themselves capable of being independent learners could opt to start their school day at second period.

Furthermore, since school is a mere reflection of the general society, school should now reflect the wired world of the 21st century where customization has rapidly become an expectation. The one-size-fits-all lesson must give way to personal choice, on-demand delivery, and customer-driven curricular options. Just as the Industrial Revolution redesigned the one-room schoolhouse to fit the factory model, the Information Revolution will redesign the traditional classroom to fit the "me" generation. There is not an app for doing that – it will take transformational school administrators.

Steve Mashburn is the coordinator of online education for the Forsyth County Schools in Cumming, Georgia. He currently works as the administrator of online content, websites, and virtual courses for his district. Steve is an educational specialist with certificates or advance degrees in technology and educational leadership. Prior to his current job, Steve was a curriculum specialist, instructional technology specialist, band director, and chorus director for numerous schools in the northern part of Georgia.

Introduction

This chapter addresses ISTE NETS.A Standard 4 "Systemic Improvement." The authors apply the latest in research in effective practices for school administrators as digital age change agents in their school districts. In the two leader reflections for this chapter, the reader finds fascinating scenarios of cutting-edge, digital age resources which are being used to support student engagement, learning, creativity, and achievement in two school districts, one in Kansas and the other in Georgia. DeYoung, in the first leader reflection, values inspiration, imagination, and innovation as qualities essential to today's school leaders. Mashburn, in the second leader reflection, has a passion for virtualization as a concept, which will change traditional ways of educating students and conducting business in the schools of the future. The NETS.A standard on systemic improvement is discussed in the following section.

Leading Organizational Change

There are two focal points of NETS.A Standard 4. First is the need for "highly competent personnel who use technology creatively." Second is the equally important need to "leverage strategic partnerships." Here are all five components of the ISTE NETS. A

Standard 4 "Systemic Improvement," including the key points on personnel and partnerships:

> Educational Administrators provide digital-age leadership and management to continuously improve the organization through the effective use of information and technology resources. Educational Administrators:
>
> (a) lead purposeful change to maximize the achievement of learning goals through the appropriate use of technology and media-rich resources;
>
> (b) collaborate to establish metrics, collect and analyze data, interpret results, and share findings to improve staff performance and student learning;
>
> (c) recruit and retain highly competent personnel who use technology creatively and proficiently to advance academic and operational goals;
>
> (d) establish and leverage strategic partnerships to support systemic improvement;
>
> (e) establish and maintain a robust infrastructure for technology including integrated, interoperable technology systems to support management, operations, teaching, and learning.
>
> (ISTE, 2009, p. 11)

Achieving Learning Goals with Technology

Educational leaders should be able to leverage digital resources in order to support instructional practices that maximize student learning (NETS.A Standard 4.a). Chapter 2 provided a thorough review of how superintendents work with district technology coordinators in order for students to perform "beyond proficiency" on district learning goals, state standards and competencies, and national assessments of educational progress. Improved student performance is linked with the use of media-rich technologies. Superintendents and curriculum coordinators should apply research to practice in the use of model academic programs in which technology is infused.

Principals can support new interactive technologies for student learning by encouraging teachers to share examples of best practice of this use in their instructional practices. In the two leader reflections at the beginning of this chapter, there is ample evidence of administrators modeling the use of wireless resources, such as handhelds for observing teachers, in order to give teachers meaningful and often quantifiable feedback on classroom interactions and student learning.

For instance, Steve Mashburn, the coordinator of online education for the Forsyth County Schools in Cumming, Georgia, comments on the risks that some school administrators might have to take in supporting the use of emerging technologies in the second leader reflection of this chapter: "Initially, five principals felt a Bring Your Own Technology (BYOT) program was worth the risks and allowed students to bring personal devices to school. These principals supported their teachers by understanding there would be a learning curve and that mistakes were bound to occur. In addition, they allowed time for teachers to assimilate greater student collaboration and project-based learning into their lessons. The principals were rewarded with greater student engagement and with less discipline issues concerning the technology (since personal devices were no longer contraband)." Risk-taking might be part of many school principals' future success with digital age tools and policies, such as BYOT, because the rewards in terms of increased student engagement and learning are great.

Data Analysis for Improved Student Learning

All school administrators need to collaborate in order to present the results of district-wide data gathering in a manner that ensures that accurate and meaningful information is collected (NETS.A Standard 4.b). Teachers do not always find that the data they receive from school administrators is helpful to them in improving their teaching practices and student learning outcomes.

Staff meetings can be used to look at data and interpret results. A high school in Iowa City, Iowa, describes a process during weekly staff meetings that pits staff members against the latest metrics of student scores. Staff members describe this transformative process, in which each member is responsible for reading the data and bringing to the staff meeting his or her interpretation of the data. But it doesn't stop there. Teachers and principals are encouraged to ask each other questions about the data and the interpretation. These Iowan educators found that looking at the data was not enough and that asking questions to help students learn was needed just as much as looking at the data itself. Could your organization benefit from something like this? Does your weekly meeting consist of examining data that could bring about systemic change in student learning? Effective assessment strategies are considered in more detail in Chapter 2.

Technology-Skilled Personnel

School district leaders should align their curriculum, learning outcomes, and technology goals as they plan for the ongoing recruitment, hiring, and evaluation of professional staff members (NETS.A Standard 4.c). The most important factor in school improvement efforts is the teachers because they are the ones who most directly affect student learning. Therefore, all teachers should have "highly qualified" status and also be proficient in the integration of digital age tools in instruction. In order to attract and retain effective faculty, superintendents and human resource directors need to use a wide array of databases in attracting new teachers.

School district administrators, for instance, need to do as much as they can to help teachers be more effective in the classroom. In turn, this means that students will be more successful. Leaders can do this by offering teachers a variety of ways in which to identify student needs. A database that is rich in history and easy to interpret offers teachers the best chance to understand student learning. Teacher candidates are becoming more and more attracted to school districts that offer a large pool of data resources. Universities and teacher education programs are promoting the use and understanding of data to better help teacher candidates teach students and identify particular student needs.

Once hired, instructional staff members can be observed and evaluated with the use of digital age technologies, such as the iPhone "app" described in one of the leader reflections at the beginning of this chapter. District-level leaders should also provide meaningful professional development for all staff in the effective use of emerging technologies. Chapter 3 provides more substantive information on teacher supervision and in-service training.

Some of the very best law firms actively recruit "top-notch" students even before they graduate from law school. They do this with attractive pay and benefits because law firms know that the return on their investment will reap larger benefits for them in the future. They are, in fact, investing in the future of their company. Why don't more school districts do the same with their technology infrastructure? One concern is the lack of highly qualified teachers. According to the State Higher Education Executive Officers (SHEEO), there are critical shortages of licensed teachers in K-12 special education, STEM subjects, and technology education (http://www.sheeo.org/quality/mobility/recruitment.pdf). This makes recruitment difficult for superintendents who wish to hire "tech-savvy" professional staff members who can create a technology vision for themselves and the students whom they will serve. This vision needs to include and embrace digital age tools that will enhance student learning. The role of the superintendent is to use technology wisely in hiring policies, job descriptions, and personnel evaluations.

But the role of the principal is essential in implementing these policies by leading the hiring, retention, and evaluation of personnel in order to attract and keep those most proficient in the use of technology to advance academic and operational goals at the building level. As DeYoung stated in his leader reflection for this chapter: "We equip our administrators with mobile technology tools to enable them to stay connected throughout their building and have real-time access to data and student information. This mobile connectivity allows them to conduct informal walk-throughs, and to stay in touch with staff instructional practices and provide just-in-time feedback to the teachers. We expect our administrators in our schools to model the use of technology to our teachers."

Strategic Partnerships

There are a variety of digital age tools that could be used to form strategic partnerships within the district and its communities in order to improve student learning (NETS.A Standard 4.d). Some of these, such as podcasts, are described in Chapter 3's leader reflections from the Hopkinton, New Hampshire, school district superintendent and principal. Other technologies that might be used by school leaders to collaborate with teachers and the local community include blogs, "tweets," wikis, social networking websites, and cloud-based Internet sites analyzed in this chapter's leader reflections. In short, effective educational leaders learn how to adapt and master rapid changes in technologies.

Establishing Partnerships

In the reflection earlier in this chapter, DeYoung elaborates upon the importance of partnerships within the school district: "It will be the three core principles embedded in our strategic technology planning and strong partnerships throughout the district that will allow us all to collectively move forward with a deeper level of technology integration in our district. All levels of staff from district administration, building administration, and teachers are needed to buy into the core principles and the technology strategic direction of the school district for technology integration. These partnerships will allow us to take policy to practice and create an innovative environment for our students to learn in." In addition to these internally based collaborations are partnerships between schools and the community, and between educational leaders and the wider online professional community.

Undoubtedly, in order for technology to work at any school, both the teacher and the administrator need to be involved. A sense of shared leadership could be the first step in implementing technology. But what else? The leader needs to provide ongoing support, identify the critical issues in technology integration, and establish priorities according to the technology plan. How can leaders, teachers, and even the community contribute to the enormous responsibility of providing leadership in technology integration in a school district? Key questions should be answered in order to develop local technology partnerships. As an administrator, one should ask:

- What are my immediate needs in developing a partnership?
- What funding sources are available to me to utilize the required change?
- What kinds of professional development can I provide for my staff?
- Will what I provide help the English language learners in my population?
- Which legal, social, and ethical issues must I be concerned with?
- What kind of technology plan can I implement?

As a teacher, one can ask these similar, but more learner-centered, questions:

- How can I partner with others to help my students?
- What support can I have with using new technologies?
- How can I use technology to enhance my instructional strategies in class?
- What could I do to impede or improve the progress of my students' learning?
- Which legal, social, and ethical issues must I be concerned with?

In one example of exemplary practice provided by the International Society for Technology in Education (ISTE), school superintendent Althea Thompson has formed a partnership with her community members and teachers through emerging technologies. She supports the district's technology plan by publishing "a blog that included the minutes from all of the meetings along with a regular podcast. The school and local community were encouraged to comment on the meeting notes and podcast throughout the process" (ISTE, 2009, p. 18). She also posts information about district activities and accomplishments on weekly blogs sent out to the community. In addition, Thomas set up a social networking site and supported her teachers in using the district's Learning Management System in order to collaborate on instructional technology integration strategies. Superintendent Thomas further models technology leadership through her involvement in an online group of superintendents who share ideas on funding distance learning initiatives for students in their small rural districts.

Resources for Partnerships

Superintendents and principals further systemic improvement by developing partnerships with multiple stakeholders within and beyond the district and its schools and communities. They promote local, national, and even global partnerships with the use of collaborative technologies. Many school principals designate one individual teacher to be the "go-to person" for technology, while other districts provide a technology coordinator because these school administrators feel uncomfortable leading technology initiatives at their sites. Perhaps it could be that they do not know how digital tools will improve learning. The traditional research in school leadership has relegated administrators to transactional functionaries. The criticism of data-driven curriculum has also emphasized the need to find ways to improve school-site scores. Yet, administrators are still expected to know about technology.

Superintendents and business administrators allocate funding and assign technology support to assist both district managerial operations and academic goals. Principals and technology coordinators also acquire, maintain, and evaluate technology resources so that dynamic and effective educational programs are supported. School leaders can use cost-effective and grant-supported methods to improve the district's cyber-infrastructure by partnering with local, state, and federal agencies. Businesses want their future employees, today's students, to have 21st-century job skills so that they will be able to compete in the global economy. Some local sources for the school leader to consider include businesses, insurance companies, department stores and Parent Teacher Associations. Other corporate sponsors might include private foundations, such as the Bill and Melinda Gates Foundation, which has supported many grants for small high-technology high schools, the Carnegie Foundation, and the Open Society Institute, which allocated several million dollars to improve urban education. On the national level, the Partnership for 21st Century Schools, founded by the U.S. Department of Education and some corporate partners in 2002, provides fiscal support for improving school technology infrastructure.

Upgrading Technology Systems

The need to have strategic planning for the integration of technology innovations and the implementation of effective interoperability standards is explored in more detail in Chapter 4. However, school district leaders, business administrators, and technology coordinators are responsible for selecting, purchasing, maintaining, and upgrading technology resources as part of the strategic plan. Existing technologies should also be evaluated as newer digital tools are investigated (NETS.A Standard 4.e).

The evaluation of management and operation systems in the district would include on-going review of administrative systems for their cost effectiveness in such operations as purchasing, transportation scheduling, and course scheduling. The maintenance of student records is another key function of management operations. In order to maintain accuracy in entering and maintaining student records, there should be regularly scheduled evaluations of currently used software programs, such as Schoolmaster Student Information Systems or PowerSchool, as well as those customized for the particular district's needs.

There are important roles for school administrators in technology systems management. Superintendents and technology coordinators must include management operability in their technology planning so that decision-making is improved at all levels in the district. For instance, technology equipment should be designed so all systems can interact with one another. The authors have talked with numerous district superintendents and technology directors across the nation who indicate that new computer systems do not interact well with older models. The benefits of interoperability are numerous; but one thing that stands out is the ability to integrate data to a global scale. A system that is interoperable can streamline data standards, improve data quality, and provide clear and instant access to much needed student data to drive instruction and the overall operations of a school or district. More detail on technology infrastructure is provided in Chapter 4.

TIPS FOR SCHOOL LEADERS

1 Use your imagination to envision future technologies in order to encourage innovative practices to improve student learning in your school.

2 Build partnerships within the district between all educators, including district and building-level administrators, to move from policy to practice in systemic change to technology integration.

3 Consider implementing a Bring Your Own Technology (BYOT) program.

4 Support the integration of social networking and Web 2.0 tools in instruction, even though there may be some challenges in terms of the need for updated acceptable use and Internet filtering policies.

5 Ensure the "virtualization" of your school district's academic operations with a Learning Management System (LMS) that will provide a variety of online courses and student special interest groups.

6 Use faculty meetings to share and interpret student test score data in order to provide intervention strategies while learning occurs.

7 Use digital age tools in developing hiring policies that attract "tech-savvy" teachers; and use emerging technologies in retaining and evaluating the most effective educators.

8 In addition to district-wide collaborations, develop partnerships between schools and the community and between educational leaders and the wider online professional community.

9 Schedule frequent evaluations of currently used software programs, such as Schoolmaster Student Information Systems or PowerSchool, in order to maintain accuracy in entering and maintaining student records.

Summary

This chapter has explored the vital role of the educational leader as change agent, supported by "tech-savvy" personnel and partnerships in technology both within and without the district. The previous four chapters have demonstrated the digital tools that can be used in professional practice by administrators and teachers alike. Leaders cannot execute systemic change alone, as they must rely on collaborative projects with technology-adept teachers. For instance, in a prior chapter you have been given the example of principals' reliance on teachers sharing their use of Web 2.0 applications in faculty meetings. Chapter 5 investigates how school leaders can continue to recruit and keep technology-adept teachers. Chapter 6 concludes with sound advice and research on how administrators can move their districts towards more digital citizenship in the 21st century.

School administrators who rate themselves and their schools or districts with scores of 5 and 4 are already meeting the standards indicated in those items. Ratings of 1 or 2 would indicate areas of needed professional growth by either the school district, or the school leader, or both in order to meet the NETS.A standards or NETP goals.

TABLE 5.1 School Administrator's Technology Leadership Self-Assessment Survey: Systemic Change with Personnel and Partnerships in Technology (Chapter 5)

Directions: Please respond to each item by circling a number from 1 to 5, where 5 = strongly agree; 4 = agree; 3 = neutral; 2 = disagree; 1 = strongly disagree.

This survey is based on National Educational Technology Standards and Performance Indicators for Administrators (NETS.A) Standard 4 (NETS.A 4.a, 4.b, 4.c, 4.d, 4.e).

5 = strongly agree (SA); 4 = agree (A); 3 = neutral (N); 2 = disagree (D); 1 = strongly disagree (SD)	SA	A	N	D	SD
1 Educational administrators in our district use digital age technology resources in order to change ineffective educational practices (NETS.A 4.a) by:					
(a) linking improved student performance with the use of media-rich technologies;	5	4	3	2	1
(b) encouraging teachers to share best practices of instructional uses of interactive technologies;	5	4	3	2	1
(c) using data-driven technology to implement school goals;	5	4	3	2	1
(d) using data-driven technology to implement the district's mission;	5	4	3	2	1
(e) using data-driven technology to implement state mandated legislation;	5	4	3	2	1
(f) using data-driven technology to implement federally mandated legislation;	5	4	3	2	1
(g) using data-driven technology to improve the dropout rate.	5	4	3	2	1

(continued)

TABLE 5.1 *(continued)*

5 = strongly agree (SA); 4 = agree (A); 3 = neutral (N); 2 = disagree (D); 1 = strongly disagree (SD)	SA	A	N	D	SD
2 Administrators in our district are collaborative users of information resources in order to improve teacher performance (NETS.A 4.b) by:					
(a) establishing metrics or competencies;	5	4	3	2	1
(b) collecting and analyzing classroom observation data;	5	4	3	2	1
(c) collecting and analyzing student achievement data;	5	4	3	2	1
(d) sharing data interpretations with teachers;	5	4	3	2	1
(e) recommending changes in instructional methods based on data results;	5	4	3	2	1
(f) encouraging differentiated instruction based on data results.	5	4	3	2	1
3 Principals and superintendent(s) in our district recruit and retain "tech-savvy" educators (NETS.A 4.c):					
(a) district-level administrators who use digital age technologies for more efficient managerial operations are hired and retained;	5	4	3	2	1
(b) principals and supervisors who use digital age technologies for advancing academic goals are hired and retained;	5	4	3	2	1
(c) highly qualified teachers who use technology resources proficiently and creatively are hired and retained.	5	4	3	2	1
4 Our district leaders support systemic improvement through strategic technology partnerships (NETS.A 4.d):					
(a) locally, with businesses in the community;	5	4	3	2	1
(b) statewide, with the state department of education;	5	4	3	2	1
(c) statewide and regionally, with professional organizations;	5	4	3	2	1
(d) statewide and regionally, with businesses;	5	4	3	2	1
(e) nationally, with federal government agencies;	5	4	3	2	1
(f) nationally, with professional organizations;	5	4	3	2	1
(g) nationally, with businesses;	5	4	3	2	1
(h) internationally, with businesses or professional organizations or online communities.	5	4	3	2	1
5 Our district has a technology-enhanced infrastructure which includes (NETS.A 4.e):					
(a) fully integrated and interoperable systems;	5	4	3	2	1
(b) secure data storage on and off site (cloud based).	5	4	3	2	1

V. E. Garland and C. Tadeja, 2012

DISCUSSION QUESTIONS

1 Make a list of organizations near your community with which you or your school can partner. In another column, describe what that relationship could look like specifically, and describe the benefits to students that this kind of relationship could bring, especially as it relates to systemic improvement. On the bottom of your paper, pick one of the organizations you selected and draw a timeline of how this kind of relationship could be solidified from possibility to reality.

2 In a small group, turn to three or four other people and discuss the possibility of leading purposeful change in your immediate or global organization. Outline a few challenges that this could bring. Make sure each person in your group contributes equally in some way and be prepared to discuss your findings with the larger group.

3 How does your organization use data? What kinds of data are analyzed and in what ways are you encouraged to make interpretations of that data and present your findings? If your organization does not participate in the use of data, what ways could data be used in your organization, especially as it relates to improving student learning?

4 Describe your organization's teacher evaluation process, especially as it relates to improving teacher performance. In what ways is the data used to recommend changes to encourage differentiated instruction?

5 In the first leader reflection for this chapter, DeYoung refers to three core ideas of "imagination," "inspiration," and "innovation" in the technology change efforts of his school district. What value do you place on these ideas? How are you and administrators in your district taking a leadership role in this type of digital age systemic change?

6 In the second leader reflection of this chapter, Mashburn comments on the use of wireless technologies to conduct teacher observations by a principal in his district: "Administrators who take the time and effort to make classroom visits to see technology-enhanced lessons have more technology-enhanced lessons in their schools. Dr. Gary Davidson of Lambert High School is one such principal. He uses an "app" on his iPhone to record his classroom visits, and emails the teacher with his observation as he is leaving the classroom." What are the most effective ways for supervisors to use wireless technologies in order to observe, evaluate, and retain "tech-savvy" teachers?

7 Based on your responses to the self-assessment for Chapter 5, what are the next steps you might take in becoming a more effective change agent in the use of digital age technologies in your school or district? What is the district lacking or proud of in terms of "tech-savvy" personnel? What technology resources would you need in your own professional e-portfolio in order to assist you in achieving your goals?

6

Legal and Social Issues in Technology

Synopsis

This final chapter incorporates the strategies needed for school leaders to assist students in becoming responsible digital citizens. Chapter 6 is fully aligned with the ISTE NETS.A Standard 5 "Digital Citizenship." In the leader reflection by John David Son, director of instructional technology for an Illinois school district, the reader will find practical advice on managing appropriate Internet uses for students. The sections which follow address concerns that administrators may have with students' interactions on school-based computers, with laws relating to copyright and Internet access, and with socially appropriate digitally based communications. Additional analysis is given on the need for ethical and environmentally sound technology practices.

Reflections of an Instructional Technology Director in Illinois

The world around us is changing at a rapid pace. Students today have access to tools, resources, and information that was not available for previous generations. As educators, we must ensure the appropriate, safe, and effective use of these tools by our students to ensure they become well-rounded digital citizens.

Many school districts today struggle with Internet filtering policies, plagiarism, and appropriate Internet use. School districts invest thousands of dollars in equipment, resources, and personnel to block inappropriate content and access. The Children's Internet Protection Act (CIPA) requires school districts to block access to such content as pornography, gambling, or obscenity. Every school district is required by law to block such content, and we do that fairly well; but what about the other content? What about the social media/networking sites? YouTube? Twitter? Facebook? Many school districts today block access to those sites because they don't want to deal with potential distractions, or incidents that *might* occur from their use. School districts spend hours each day searching log files, blocking new sites, and disciplining students according to acceptable use policies. Wouldn't a better use of our time, energy, and resources be educating our students [on] how to *appropriately* utilize these tools to enhance their educational experience?

A better utilization of our time as educators and a better outcome for our students would be to focus on educating students [on] how to appropriately and effectively utilize these tools to enhance their communication, collaboration, and productivity. Students today struggle with understanding how the content and material they place on the web can impact their future. They don't comprehend how an image or comment can be viewed three to five years later by an employer or university, which could have a significant impact on their future. As educators, we should be teaching our students how to utilize these tools both inside our walls and outside. In order to do so, students have to have access. Obviously, as with any institution or environment, you will have some who choose to abuse the privilege they are given. But why deny access to the majority, when the minority chooses to abuse? Educate all and allow those who choose to disobey rules, regulations, and teachings to suffer appropriate consequences.

School districts today must have appropriate acceptable use guidelines for overall communication practices for both students and teachers. Districts need to outline appropriate and inappropriate utilization of communication tools, such as text messaging, social networking, email, and even voice communication. By providing best practice guidelines, students and teachers are able to reduce risks, and utilize the appropriate tool for the appropriate time and conversation. Keeping parents informed and engaged during these conversations is critical. Allow parents the opportunity to provide feedback and guidance on the process and how they view the communication between a student and teacher at all grade levels. School districts today must take a strong position when it comes to cyber bullying. Educating our students and teachers on what cyber bullying looks like, where it takes place, and what the consequences are when it occurs provides opportunities for conversations and discussions between educator and student. This has to be an embedded part of every school district's curriculum – at all grade levels. The earlier we start educating our students on what is appropriate and safe, the less likely they are to take part in inappropriate actions. We cannot wait until students are in junior high or high school to begin our education programs; it is too late. These conversations and discussions must start at the elementary levels, with grade-appropriate topics, building upon each other.

In Naperville District 203, we partner with the local Naperville Police Department through our Learning Resource Centers to provide a comprehensive education program that spans grades 3 to 12. Our elementary schools have developed a curriculum that is reviewed and updated on an annual basis. Students at the junior high and high school level apply the concept of digital citizenship throughout the regular curriculum during projects and assignments. They also discuss and review appropriate Internet safety and digital citizenship concepts with school resource officers throughout the school year. As a district, we keep our parents, community, and school board abreast of our continued growth in this area through community seminars, anti-cyber bullying campaigns, web-based content, and partnering with our student government associations.

Naperville District 203 has also invested significant time and resources to the development of our *Electronic Communication Guidelines*. These guidelines were developed through focus groups of students, teachers, administrators, and parents. The guidelines are intended to, first, provide best practices for teachers and students to communicate and collaborate with one another regarding district/school business; and, second, provide a safe and secure vehicle to allow the utilization of Web 2.0 social networking tools in the classroom for instructional purposes – where appropriate. This represents a significant step forward for our district in allowing the appropriate utilization of communication and collaboration tools that extend [beyond] the walls of our classrooms and create a global education community for teachers and students.

We as educators must be active in the digital education of our students. We cannot rely on the world, web, or peers to educate them on these matters. Creating a culture of safe, smart, and secure digital citizens is a responsibility of every school district across this great nation. Students today live on these tools. If you remove access it doesn't enhance their learning: it inhibits their creativity, collaboration, and communication. Teach them how to appropriately use it in the classroom and enable the technology in their lives to enrich the learning experience. They are our future, and they deserve the appropriate education and understanding on what it means to be a true digital citizen.

John David Son is currently the director of instructional technology for Naperville Community School District 203 in Naperville, Illinois. Naperville is approximately 30 miles west of Chicago and the school district serves nearly 20,000 students in 21 schools, from kindergarten to high school. Prior to this, John was a chief information officer and public relations director in Benton, Kentucky, where he was responsible for a large Management Learning System and successfully installed and implemented complete wireless coverage for all schools in the district. Naperville Community School District is consistently ranked high in student achievement by the U.S. News & World Report, *the* Chicago Tribune, Chicago Magazine, *and the* Chicago Sun Times *and is consistently ranked among the top ten largest school districts in Illinois.*

Introduction

This chapter addresses ISTE NETS.A Standard 5 "Digital Citizenship." You have read in the leader reflection how the appropriate use of social networking tools for educational purposes can be of value to student learning and creativity. The reader will also have the opportunity to review key laws and guidelines for making students safe and "savvy" digital citizens in the next sections. The chapter concludes with ideas for more ethical and global collaborations.

Digital Citizenship

Superintendents, principals, and technology coordinators lead the district in digital citizenship by modeling and supporting best practices in social interactions, ethical practices, and legally appropriate uses of technology by students, staff, and administrators. These leadership roles are further defined in the four components of ISTE NETS.A Standard 5 "Digital Citizenship":

> Educational Administrators model and facilitate understanding of social, ethical, and legal issues and responsibilities related to an evolving digital culture.
>
> Educational Administrators:
>
> (a) ensure equitable access to appropriate digital tools and resources to meet the needs of all learners;
>
> (b) promote, model, and establish policies for safe, legal, and ethical use of digital information and technology;
>
> (c) promote and model responsible social interactions related to the use of technology and information;
>
> (d) promote and facilitate the development of a shared cultural understanding and involvement in global issues through the use of contemporary communication and collaboration tools.
>
> (ISTE, 2009, p. 11)

School Leaders as Digital Citizens

Exemplary superintendents, principals, and technology coordinators who advance the use of technology in their organization empower learning in the 21st century. As reviewed in Chapter 4, educational leaders do not need to have the most advanced technology infrastructure in their own districts. But they do need to be able to assess how emerging technologies can leverage real learning for all students; and they do have to be able to find the resources to achieve and sustain this goal (NETS.A Standard 5). Their leadership in embracing digital age tools, especially those in the area of how students communicate, sets a tone for the way in which technology is carried out in the district.

Throughout this book, we have seen that technology is key to the success of school leaders because it is the catalyst for organizational changes, which will propel student performance. The superintendents and principals whom the authors spoke to from across the country started out as classroom teachers. They do not easily forget the challenges and great responsibilities that come with teaching. But coupled with that past experience is the idea of teaching tomorrow's 21st-century learner and how technology now plays a critical role in the way that students learn. The digital age can become especially challenging to those who may be unprepared to lead teachers and students.

In modeling and facilitating understanding of a digital culture, superintendents and other leaders need to be using technology that is both appropriate and useful. Email is perhaps the easiest way to do this. Principals, technology coordinators, and district-level administrators whom the authors spoke to use email on a daily basis but not just to communicate information. They use it to provide resources and to share links to help students learn and teachers teach. As we have seen in the chapters throughout this book, the use of social media has also changed the culture in which we communicate as a learning organization. We have seen in the leader reflections how many districts now open and use Twitter and Facebook accounts to showcase student success. Principals and superintendents are embracing these social networking sites and have even been known to communicate purposefully on district issues. However, the public has criticized some school administrators for being too wordy or too lofty on these social networking sites, especially in blogging and twittering. As previously discussed, leaders do not need to comment on everything happening in their respective organizations, nor do they need to air out all of the problems that are centered in their districts. A balance of discretion and prudence is advised.

Equitable Access to Digital Tools

All school leaders must be wary in bringing about a change in the digital culture so that equity remains part of the equation in deploying the use of new technologies (NETS.A Standard 5.a). Principals, technology coordinators, and superintendents must close the digital divide. Because there could be an immediate arena of the "haves" and the "have nots" in learner access to digital age tools, school administrators need to be able to carefully distribute technology resources.

Above all, student learning should be at the forefront of what we do as educators. Any technology should be implemented with the goal of growth in student learning. Equitable access to appropriate digital tools to meet the needs of all learners is critical. Socio-economic, ethnic, racial, language, and gender factors cause this digital divide in American education. Therefore, superintendents, principals, and technology coordinators must establish guidelines that ensure that digital tools and resources are available to the diverse needs of all learners, including those who speak a language other than English or who may not have access to technology outside of the school. In addition, students who are disabled should be provided with adaptive or assistive technologies.

The advent of the Common Core Standards is becoming prevalent in more and more states across the county. At the heart of the Common Core Standards is the curriculum that is designed to bridge the gap between standards and assessments. To help support the development of this curriculum, the Bill and Melinda Gates Foundation recently invested more than $20 million in gaming, gaming simulation, and other digital tools to help students achieve the standards. This is one example of a funding source for which educational leaders can apply in order to have the technologies their students need to meet the Common Core Standards of their respective states. As the Bill and Melinda Gates Foundation's criteria for this type of funding suggests, it is necessary to address how technology can help students learn to read and write effectively and to understand math concepts more clearly. In order to achieve equity, school leaders need to establish similar guidelines that address English language learners (ELLs) and other digitally disadvantaged student populations.

In particular, principals and technology coordinators support classroom assistance and professional development for teachers in implementing new technology resources for the targeted learning needs of all students. Even though there is an increase in wireless devices for Internet access globally, equity and access to these new digital tools are issues across American schools (Garland, 2010a). For instance, Hohlfeld et al. (2008) found statistically significant disparities in levels of technology support between high and low socio-economic status schools in a study of Florida K-12 schools. Creighton (2003) confirms that higher-order technology use has decreased in low-performing schools due to the provisions of the No Child Left Behind Act, which has pressured teachers to raise standardized test scores through traditional drill and practice methods of "teaching to the test." This federal legislation has been widely criticized for not measuring students' problem-solving skills. However, as we have seen in Chapter 2, the most effective methods of instruction include media-rich, project-based learning through new technologies. It is thus imperative that educational leaders are aware of the limits of the testing provisions of the No Child Left Behind Act. School administrators should have a balance of meeting the adequate yearly progress (AYP) requirements of the law, while they actively pursue the use of digital age tools for meeting the needs of all learners, such as those in property-poor areas or special populations of students who might need adaptive technologies.

Special needs and ELL students are not always well served by the technology available in most schools because most software programs and Internet search sites are only in English. Ono and Zavodny (2008) found that students who live in Spanish-speaking homes are less likely than their English-speaking home peers to have access to information communications. Learning disabled students are also found to be academically excluded from information communications (McKenzie, 2007). Garland (2010a, pp. 40–41) found that "Other special needs learners are in need of assistive technologies that may be too expensive for some school district budgets. The availability of appropriate software and information technologies in the educational setting is thus invaluable for both English language and special needs learners."

In addition to these socio-economic, language, and special needs issues in the digital divide are factors of race and gender. In 2008, Jackson et al. conducted a study of 515 children, including 172 African Americans and 343 Caucasian Americans. They determined that: "African American males were the least intense users of computers and the Internet, and African American females were the most intense users of the Internet. Males, regardless of race, were the most intense video game players, and females, regardless of race, were the most intense cell phone users [. . .]. Length of time using computers and the Internet was a positive predictor of academic performance, whereas amount of time spent playing video games was a negative predictor" (Jackson et al., 2008, p. 437). Some studies suggest that adolescent females of all races are more likely than males to use cell phones and social networking sites; yet they are only a small proportion of those taking the advanced placement test in computers/technology (Garland, 2010a). This research informs educational leaders, enabling to be proactive proponents of equity in the use of digital age tools by all students.

Legal and Safe Policies for Technology Use

Superintendents, principals, and technology coordinators must regularly review and establish district and school policies on filtering, acceptable use, and guidelines for accessing online resources, with advice from legal experts (NETS.A Standard 5.b). Principals are leaders in the collaborative effort of teachers and administrators and parents in ensuring safe, ethical, and legal use of digital information and online resources by students in their schools.

Technology has come with a great expanse of information. Because of growing concerns of how computerized data might be affecting individuals' privacy rights, the first comprehensive law on data protection was created with the Privacy Act of 1974. Since then, numerous laws and safeguards have been put in place to ensure that individuals' rights are protected. Today, privacy issues can be as simple as password protection updates or as complex as the use, transmission, sharing, and deleting of data such as student records.

Acceptable Use Policy (AUP)

The starting point for every school district is to have an acceptable use policy (AUP), which outlines how its networked system is to be accessed and used. It is generally common practice for newly hired employees of the school or district to sign an agreement with the AUP. This document should be simple and easily read by all parents and community members. The Los Angeles Unified School District is the second largest school district in the nation and so one might think that its AUP would be lengthy and monotonous to read. However, it is only one page, outlining in simple terms what is expected when one uses its network. It also gives the user, in very simple terms, the penalties for breaking such rules, all condensed into one paragraph. At the bottom of their AUP is a place for users to sign an agreement with its conditions (http://notebook.lausd.net/portal/page?_pageid=33,136640&_dad=ptl&_schema= ptl_ep).

Here are some suggestions for designing an acceptable use policy in your school or district:

1 Keep it simple, one page if possible.

2 Use student-friendly language, but be very clear about the policies.

3 Provide reasons for having the AUP.

4 Install penalties for misuse.

5 Have a place for all stakeholders to sign an agreement with the AUP requirements.

Compliance training conducted yearly for all staff members could minimize any possible negative impact upon the way in which the acceptable use policy is carried out in the district. Technology changes constantly on a yearly, if not sooner, basis. It makes sense, therefore, to institute a training program that is updated frequently. This way, stakeholders from the district can be trained or retrained in the latest technology, acceptable uses, or other policy decisions that could have an impact upon the way in which the district or school site is run.

Children's Internet Protection Act (CIPA)

The Children's Internet Protection Act (CIPA) was implemented in 2001 to ensure that all school districts had a federally mandated Internet safety policy in place in order to prevent children under 18 years of age from accessing inappropriate material on the web while in school. Subsequent to that law, both the nation's state attorneys general and the social networking site MySpace collaborated to keep children safe from sexual predators (Garland, 2010a). School principals are thus required to have safe Internet use policies in place at the building level that meet both state and federal mandates. In 2008, the Broadband Data Improvement Act was passed, providing state grants for broadband initiatives at the state level and an amendment to CIPA. The CIPA amendment added updated requirements for schools' online safety policies, including appropriate interactions on social networking websites and awareness of cyber bullying. School districts that fail to meet the provisions of CIPA lose E-Rate and/or No Child Left Behind Act (NCLB) federal funding.

Copyright Issues

School administrators must enforce fair use of the Copyright Act in order not to commit copyright infringement: "However, this is a challenge due to the increase in the socially accepted practices of uploading and downloading of creative works without permission. Because the proliferation of wireless devices allows easy access to the Internet and social networking sites, students frequently and perhaps innocently engage in online theft by taking copyrighted images and music through search engines such as Google and post them to their Facebook or MySpace web pages" (Garland, 2010a, p. 44). Nevertheless, the copyright law does allow teachers and students to use some material for educational purposes within the classroom. Without written consent, students and teachers who use copyrighted text, graphics, music, and images from the web may only do so in the classroom and such work cannot be displayed in the school district or on the web (Baker, 2008). Understanding copyright laws is quite complex and the topic of copyright extends beyond pictures and images.

Created in 2002, Creative Commons is an alternative way to address some of the existing problems of copyrighted material. Nearly everything found on the Internet is copyrighted; but Creative Commons presents a few ways in which authors can share their material, including duration and to what extent. As students and teachers begin to utilize various Web 2.0 tools, it will be important for them to understand the extent of the materials that they use or gather for their own projects from the Internet. Multiple forms of media including images, sounds, podcasts, and screencasts have some sort of copyright protection and because copyright can affect more than the individual when used in a school setting, it is important to utilize a service such as Creative Commons to avoid any potential issues regarding copyright. Other websites that have been used include iStockPhoto.com, which houses numerous stock photography that is both royalty free and uses Creative Commons licensing. Consider also EFF.org, FreeSound.org, and MagnaTune.com, all of which are non-profit organizations for aspiring musicians and audio-visual lovers and which also use Creative Commons licensing. Technology coordinators are often the ones who enforce these copyright laws by ensuring that student multimedia projects in which there are copyrighted materials do not appear on school district or classroom websites. School administrators should have clear, enforceable policies in place that require copyrighted materials, which do not have Creative Commons licensing, to only be used in classrooms for one-time-only student projects.

Cell Phone Policies

Districts also need to have clear policies for student use of cell phones: Privacy issues exist in relation to smartphones' photographic, video streaming, and texting capabilities. Obringer and Coffey (2007) found that smartphones allow students to "cheat" on exams by photographing or texting answers, and infringe on student privacy (perhaps committing sexual harassment) by taking photographs in school locker rooms. Cell phones may be valuable for emergencies or after school events; but many schools have developed polices which prohibit the use of smartphones during school hours. Smartphones have recently been clouded in controversy regarding students' use of their photographic capabilities to cheat on exams or projects. However, there are also documented cases around the country and in parts of England where the use of smartphones is being allowed in schools. Administrators and teachers have found valuable ways to utilize information that is communicated on smartphones, such as the location of an intruder in the building. Many schools require that students who "bring their own devices" or Bring Your Own Technology (BYOT) must connect to the school's network, which filters out inappropriate and social media websites. The use of BYOT is discussed in more detail in Chapter 5.

Internet Filtering

Internet content filtering is the law in schools, and it is becoming more commonplace in organizations that want to limit the amount of information gleaned from the Internet. Schools are becoming more adept at using their filtering programs, which can now predict inappropriate online student behavior based on previous search terms and websites visited. A school district in Tulsa, Oklahoma, has made use of Gaggle, which provides a suite of online learning tools. Gaggle allows the use of YouTube by filtering it to admit only the safest content. Teachers and administrators are now realizing the positive possibilities that reside in using videos from YouTube and other commonly blocked sites. Other sites include TeacherTube, Khan Academy, and other video-propelled websites. These websites provide a trove of learning opportunities through videos that offer different or additional perspectives. Learning the origins of the universe, how calculus works in the real world, or even seeing an example of pig dissection can all be found in numerous YouTube videos. But because the videos appear on this website, many schools simply refuse to allow access to it despite its inherent and obvious educational value. Gaggle allows users to access many of these materials since it has already pre-filtered the videos. Pre-filtering digital age tools can be valuable for teachers to engage learners, while meeting legal constraints imposed by the CIPA legislation.

Internet filtering is a valuable, yet not necessarily a required, part of the Internet surfing culture. District firewalls, which are also used to catch inappropriate or unwanted material, are other ways to filter out information. One further resource for school leaders to consider is the i-SAFE website, which educates children on the perils and dangers of online behavior. This website sets standards for Internet safety education, but also reaches out to the community by educating educators, teachers, parents, law enforcement, and others about safe practices for Internet use. This is a strongly recommended website and offers both print and videos for local-level to global-level use.

Cyber Bullying

In order to promote safe student engagement, superintendents, principals, and technology coordinators need to implement policies and model the appropriate social interactions in the use of other digital age technologies, including blogging, twittering, and texting. There should be clearly stated and shared district policies regarding filtering and acceptable use of social networking sites in order to avoid sexual predators and cyber bullying.

Perhaps one of the biggest social media challenges today is the way in which we address the issue of cyber bullying. There is little doubt about the critical role that social networks play in the social and emotional maturation of today's children. Because of the speed in which children can access social media, online identify has become a modern form of electronic communication (Snakenborg, et al., 2011). Thus, the issue of cyber bullying, which many consider to be another form of traditional bullying, can manifest itself quickly.

Cyber bullying is a big problem and continues to grow each year. Perhaps the best way to combat this issue is to first address the boundaries that can support and prevent the spread of cyber bullying amongst children. District leaders need to ask important questions about how involved they will get with student activities. Principals and school site administrators need to be able to identify and prioritize their top concerns. Finally, district officials and even school sites should provide continual professional development to address the growing and complex issue of cyber bullying. Does your school site have a Professional Learning Community to address these issues? Is the principal alone left to deal with this topic or are there others, including teachers and the community, committed to eradicating this destructive behavior?

School leaders must protect their students from these predators and cyber bullies, while at the same time encouraging the educational uses of social networking tools. According to Dillon (2008), an editor of the *American School Board Journal*, a majority of all high school students reported being the victims of cyber bullying. Dillon encourages all school districts to have cyber bullying polices in place, while also finding "ways to harness the educational value of social networking. Some schools and educators are experimenting successfully with chat rooms, instant messaging, blogs, wikis, and more for after-school homework help, review sessions, and collaborative projects, for example" (Dillon, 2008, p16).

As administrators and educational leaders, it is important to establish guidelines, as in traditional bullying, to better address how an organization will deal with cyber bullying issues. Although there are numerous ways in which to address this issue, the following are perhaps some of the most effective ways to prevent the phenomenon.

Administrators should clearly establish rules surrounding the use of electronic media and how it is employed in the organization. Many school organizations now use an acceptable use policy that guides the use of electronic media and technology for both students and adults. The Children's Internet Protection Act is a federal law enacted by Congress to address concerns about access that children have to the Internet. One of the requirements of CIPA is for schools and libraries to adopt a policy to monitor online activities of students.

Prevention can also be taken with the establishment of curricular programs to address the issue of cyber bullying. One-time or long-term courses on Internet safety are something that organizations can initiate to educate students about this ever growing issue. Classes could include discussions on topics regarding cyber bullying, invasion of personal/private information, and Internet safety. There are a number of curriculum-based programs that can help to address these issues with organizations and many states have already established curriculums designed to meet this need.

Technological advances can also assist in the issue of cyber bullying. Websites such as Facebook, MySpace, Twitter, and other social networking sites have links that can easily allow the user to report site abuse. Search engines that list unwanted information can be contacted to disable that information. Any information about children under the age of 13 can be removed from any website as this violates the Children's Online Privacy Protection Act and the Federal Trade Commission's guidelines.

Social Issues in Technology Use

Social issues in technology use by students and educators involve not only safety and privacy but also sound ethical and communication practices (NETS.A Standard 5.c). There are also environmental concerns that are raised with the non-ethical ways of disposing of the technology hardware no longer used by many schools. For instance, in order to properly dispose of schools' old computers, which are comprised of toxins, ecologically sound practices should be followed. Motavalli (2007, p. 59) reported that flame-retardants used in the plastic housing of computers, FAX machines, printers, and circuit boards are highly toxic in "Taizhou, China, where much of the digital detritus from our computerized society ends up. Instead of eco-correct dismantling, you'll see workers exposed to myriad toxins as they bang computers apart with primitive hammers. This is the dark side of Being Digital." Since millions of computers become obsolete each year in schools across the country, school leaders should be practicing environmentally appropriate technology waste removal. They can do this by research-ing and finding companies that will safely remove and destroy or recycle old computers or other obsolete hardware, such as FAX machines and copiers.

Cross-Cultural and Global Collaborations

Superintendents, principals, and technology coordinators should work with represen-tatives of diverse cultures and nationalities in encouraging global connections between both education professionals and their students (NETS.A Standard 5.d). There are best practices in this need to establish social connections between educational professionals and their students on a worldwide basis. For instance, social networking tools were invaluable educational and political tools in the social and governmental changes of the 2011 "Arab spring" of student protests in the Middle East.

Some schools have used technologies such as Polycom, or they have expanded the use of Skype to communicate with other learning communities across the globe. With cost-cutting measures becoming more commonplace in today's educational system, a link to other school communities gives students a much needed perspective that is sometimes missing in the classroom of today. Students in one community in Winchester, Massachusetts, for instance, can use this kind of system to speak and collaborate with other students on projects in Winchester, Nevada, or even as far away as Winchester, England. Providing students with these types of opportunities to collaborate with other students allows for an effective and enriching cross-cultural experience.

TIPS FOR SCHOOL LEADERS

1 Here are some important questions to ask before developing a cyber bullying policy for your school or district:

   (a) What issues are prompting the updating or creation of an anti-cyber bullying policy?

   (b) What does the district or school website currently define as cyber bullying?

   (c) What are my top concerns as a superintendent or principal about cyber bullying?

   (d) What staff development training will I provide to address this topic?

   (e) What resources, including experts, do I have to initiate or sustain an effective anti-cyber bullying policy?

2 Make sure that your school district is in full compliance with the Children's Internet Protection Act (CIPA), which requires that students are blocked access to such content as pornography, gambling, or obscenity.

3 Provide clear guidelines on the appropriate and inappropriate utilization of social networking tools for educational purposes, particularly the social networking communication tools of text messaging, filming, emailing, and posting information on Internet-based sites.

4 Have strong anti-cyber bullying policies by educating not only teachers but also students and their parents on the forms of cyber bullying that can occur at all grade levels.

5 Discuss and review appropriate Internet safety and digital citizenship with school resource officers throughout the school year.

6 Encourage teachers and students to explore and to collaborate with the global world of Internet users by safely and securely using Web 2.0 social networking tools.

7 Overcome the socio-economic, disability, ethnic, racial, language, and gender factors that can cause a digital divide in your school or district by providing equitable access to appropriate technology resources for all learners.

8 Ensure simplicity and clarity as you design an acceptable use policy (AUP) in your school or district by using student-friendly language which includes the purpose, the penalties for misuse, and a place for all stakeholders to sign an agreement with the guidelines.

9 Enforce fair use of the Copyright Act by not allowing students and teachers to use copyrighted text, graphics, music, and images from the web outside of the classroom without written consent.

10 Use only "green" companies in order to safely remove and destroy or recycle old computers or other obsolete hardware such as FAX machines and copiers.

11 Provide your students with opportunities to collaborate with other students around the world for enriching cross-cultural experiences.

Summary

In Chapter 1, the need for strategic planning to integrate technology innovations was explored. Chapter 2 provided a critical review of best practices in embedding technology in instructional and assessment practices. Excellence in professional practice was the theme of Chapter 3, with a discussion of how digital tools can facilitate communication and collaboration in schools and their communities. Chapter 4 provided an analysis of professional development opportunities for administrators and teachers regarding new technologies. In Chapter 5, the role of the leader as change agent through personnel and partnerships was explored. In this final chapter, suggestions are given to the school administrator on implementing updated acceptable use and Internet safety policies. Chapter 6 concludes with remarks from the authors on the vital need to apply emerging 21st-century technologies in order to improve student learning, both nationally and globally.

School administrators who rate themselves and their schools or districts with scores of 5 and 4 are already meeting the standards indicated in those items. Ratings of 1 or 2 would indicate areas of needed professional growth by either the school district, or the school leader, or both in order to meet the NETS.A standards or NETP goals.

TABLE 6.1 School Administrator's Technology Leadership Self-Assessment Survey: Legal and Social Issues in Technology (Chapter 6)

Directions: Please respond to each item by circling a number from 1 to 5, where 5 = strongly agree; 4 = agree; 3 = neutral; 2 = disagree; 1 = strongly disagree.

This survey is based on National Educational Technology Standards and Performance Indicators for Administrators (NETS.A) Standard 5 (NETS.A 5.a, 5.b, 5.c, 5.d).

5 = strongly agree (SA); 4 = agree (A); 3 = neutral (N); 2 = disagree (D); 1 = strongly disagree (SD)	SA	A	N	D	SD
1 Educational administrators in our district set and achieve goals for equity in the availability of digital age tools and resources for all students and professional staff members (NETS.A 5.a) by:					
(a) providing equal access to technology resources for all students;	5	4	3	2	1
(b) providing appropriate access to technology resources and training for all teachers and professional staff members;	5	4	3	2	1
(c) supporting learning opportunities for all students with digital age technology tools.	5	4	3	2	1
2 Educational administrators in our district implement policies for safe, legal, and ethical uses of technology information (NETS.A 5.b) by:					
(a) establishing, monitoring, and enforcing a technology "acceptable use" Internet policy for students, teachers, and all employees;	5	4	3	2	1
(b) promoting "online safety" for all students and employees;	5	4	3	2	1
(c) providing students and staff with training on the ethical uses of technology, including issues such as inappropriate websites and plagiarism;	5	4	3	2	1
(d) fully enforcing copyright laws associated with technology use of intellectual property;	5	4	3	2	1
(e) fully complying with the provisions of the Children's Internet Protection Act (CIPA);	5	4	3	2	1
(f) promoting "environmentally safe" technology practices, such as recycling and conserving paper.	5	4	3	2	1
3 Educational administrators in our district allow only those social interactions with technologies in the schools that are educationally appropriate (NETS.A 5.c) by:					
(a) establishing effective anti-cyber bullying policies;	5	4	3	2	1
(b) fully enforcing anti-cyber bullying policies.	5	4	3	2	1

5 = strongly agree (SA); 4 = agree (A); 3 = neutral (N); 2 = disagree (D); 1 = strongly disagree (SD)	SA	A	N	D	SD
4 Educational administrators in our district use digital age technologies to promote cross-cultural and multinational collaboration (NETS.A 5.d) by:					
(a) online partnerships that foster cross-cultural collaborations;	5	4	3	2	1
(b) engagement in professional organizations which have international membership;	5	4	3	2	1
(c) student use of digital age tools to engage with learners from other nations.	5	4	3	2	1

V. E. Garland and C. Tadeja, 2012

DISCUSSION QUESTIONS

1 Does your school or school district block content? What do you know about this process? Who determines what information is to be blocked? Using a diagram, draw a representation of the kinds of information your school or school district blocks (or can block) and the positive or negative impact this can create for student learning. Be sure to include the benefits and possible consequences of this kind of blocking. Be prepared to share findings with the rest of the group.

2 Discuss with a small group (or draft a paper on) what content should be included in establishing, monitoring, and enforcing an acceptable use policy (AUP) for your organization. Discuss the need to protect intellectual property as it relates to an AUP.

3 Identify several scenarios in which cyber bullying could take place between students and other students and/or employees and other employees. Be prepared to discuss these scenarios as well as their possible solutions with other individuals and/or groups.

4 With what other professional organizations could you partner? How would you promote and foster cross-cultural collaboration? How would you engage in multinational collaboration? What could you do to sustain such a relationship?

5 In the leader reflection for this chapter, John David Son states: "The Children's Internet Protection Act (CIPA) requires school districts to block access to such content as pornography, gambling, or obscenity. Every school district is required by law to block such content, and we do that fairly well; but what about the other content? What about the social media/networking sites? YouTube? Twitter? Facebook? Many school districts today block access to those sites because they don't want to deal with potential distractions, or incidents that *might* occur from their use. School districts spend hours each

day searching log files, blocking new sites, and disciplining students according to acceptable use policies. Wouldn't a better use of our time, energy, and resources be educating our students [on] how to *appropriately* utilize these tools to enhance their educational experience?" Discuss concerns you might have with enforcing the CIPA and your agreement or disagreement with Son's ideas on student access and appropriate educational uses of Internet-based social networking tools.

6 Based on your responses to the self-assessment for Chapter 6, what are the next steps you might take in becoming a more effective leader in the educational use of social networking tools in your school or district? What is the district lacking or proud of in terms of safe Internet access or cyber bullying policies or environmentally sound practices? What technology resources would you need in your own professional e-portfolio in order to assist you in achieving your goals?

Concluding Remarks

This textbook is designed to help the educational leader with following the NETS.A standards and NETP goals for implementing technology in his or her school or district. Although the technology that is available now will soon be replaced by even more advanced digital tools, this book outlines an engagement with best practices in technology use for school principals, technology coordinators, and superintendents. It also serves the needs of pre-service or in-service administrators, as well as teachers, technology coordinators, and even district-level officials.

Perhaps the biggest recent change in technology use is the adaptation of social networking tools to instructional purposes. The ways in which teachers communicate with students today differ substantially from 20, 10, or even just a few years ago. Could you imagine a world that never used or had even heard of texting, blogging, "Likes," or the hash mark? It is commonplace today for school administrators to send out an email or online newsletter or blog to parents and the community, letting them know about events taking place. Parents no longer wait for the obligatory one night where they come to the school to get the latest information on their children's academic progress. Instead, instant digital age communications are widely used and involve more stakeholders in the educational process on a broader, even global, scale. What will come next? What new technologies will we see? As current or future school leaders, we hope that you, the reader, will find some answers to these key issues and will be better prepared for the 21st-century's digital age.

References

Baker, J. (2008) "Ethics: Schools teach students about copyright laws," *Bowling Green Daily News* (KY), 19 November.

Bogler, R. (2005) "The power of empowerment: Mediating the relationship between teachers' participation in decision making and their professional commitment," *Journal of School Leadership*, 15, pp76–98.

Brooks-Young, S. (2006) *Critical Technology Issues for School Leaders*, Thousand Oaks, CA: Corwin Press.

Brooks-Young, S. (2009) *Making Technology Standards Work for You*, 2nd edition. Eugene, OR: International Society for Technology in Education.

Cavanaugh, C. (2009) "Effectiveness of cyber charter schools: A review of research on learnings," *TechTrends: Linking Research and Practice to Improve Learning*, 53(4), pp28–31.

Christensen, C. M., Horn, M. B., and Johnson, C. W. (2008) *Disrupting Cass: How Disruptive Innovation Will Change the Way the World Learns*, New York, NY: McGraw-Hill.

Connecticut Department of Higher Education (2011) *Higher Education Counts: Achieving Results, 2011*, Report, Connecticut: Connecticut Department of Higher Education.

Creighton, T. (2003) *The Principal as Technology Leader*, Thousand Oaks, CA: Corwin Press, Inc.

Davis, M. (2009) "Web-based classes booming in schools," *Education Week*, 28(19), p. 5.

Dede, C. (2009) "Immersive interfaces for engagement and learning," *Science*, 323, pp66–69.

Dees, D., Mayer, A., Morin, H., and Willis, E. (2010) "Librarians as leaders in professional learning communities through technology, literacy, and collaboration," *Library Media Connection*, 29(2), pp10–13.

Demski, J. (2010) "Ed tech experts choose top tools," *T.H.E. Journal*, 37(7), pp32–37.

Dessoff, A. (2009) "Reaching graduation with credit recovery," *District Administration*, 45(9), pp43–48.

Dieterle, E. (2009) "Neomillenial learning styles and River City," *Children, Youth and Environments*, 19(1), pp245–278.

Dillon, N. (2008) "A tangled web," *American School Board Journal*, 195(12), December, pp14–17.

DuFour, R., DuFour, R., Eaker, R., and Karhanek, G. (2010) *Raising the Bar and Closing the Gap*, Bloomington, IN: Solution Tree.

Economides, A. A. (2008) "Culture-aware collaborative learning," *Multicultural Education and Technology Journal*, 2(4), pp243–267.

Feng, M., Heffernan, N., and Koedinger, K. (2009) "Addressing the assessment challenge in an online system that tutors as it assesses," *User Modeling and User-Adapted Interaction: The Journal of Personalization Research (UMUAI)*, 19(3), pp243–266.

Ferriter, W. and Garry, A. (2010) *Teaching the iGeneration*, Bloomington, IN: Solution Tree.

Frommelt, D. (2009) *Augmented Reality*, Penn State Web 2009 Class Presentation.

Garland, V. E. (2006) "Digital literacy and the use of wireless portable computers, planners, and cell phones for K-12 education," in L. Hin and R. Subramaniam (eds) *Literacy in Technology at the K-12 Level: Issues and Challenges*, Hershey, US: Idea Group Publishing, pp308–321.

Garland, V. E. (2008) "Transforming instruction: The roles of the principal as technology leader," *Scholar and Educator*, XXIX, (1–2), pp35–45.

Garland, V. E. (2009) "Wireless technologies and multimedia literacies for K-12 education," in L. Hin and R. Subramaniam (eds) *Handbook of Research on New Media Literacy at the K-12 Level*, Hershey, US: IGI Global, pp471–479.

Garland, V. E. (2010a) "Emerging technology trends and ethical practices for the school principal," *Journal of Educational Technology Systems*, 38(1), pp39–50.

Garland, V. E. (2010b) "The hybrid online course: Best practices," Paper presented to the Annual Conference of the Society of Educators and Scholars, San Antonio, TX, October.

Garland, V. E. (2011) "Leading the online school," in S. Huffman, S. Albritton, B. Wilmes, and W. Rickman (eds) *Cases on Building Quality Distance Delivery Programs*, Hershey, US: IGI Global, pp109–121.

Genachowski, J. (2011) *Prepared Remarks at the Minority Media & Telecom Council Broadband and Social Justice Summit*, Washington, DC: Federal Communications Commission, http://fjallfoss.fcc.gov/edocs_public/attachmatch/DOC-304191A1.txt.

Gulbahar, Y. (2007) "Technology planning: A roadmap to successful technology integration in schools," *Computers and Education*, 49(4), pp943–956.

Heaton-Shrestha, C., May, S., and Burke, L. (2009) "Student retention in higher education: What role for virtual learning environments?," *Journal of Further and Higher Education*, 33(1), pp83–92.

Herbert, M. (2010) "Big steps for National Education Technology Plan," *District Administration*, 46(5), p. 12.

Hohlfeld, T., Ritzhaupt, A., Barron, A., and Kemker, K. (2008) "Examining the digital divide in K-12 public schools: Four-year trends for supporting ICT literacy in Florida," *Computers and Education*, 51(4), December, pp1648–1663.

Hokanson, B., Miller, C., and Hooper, S. R. (2008) "Role-based design: A contemporary perspective for innovation in instructional design," *TechTrends: Linking Research and Practice to Improve Learning*, 52(6), pp36–43.

Howe, N. and Strauss, W. (2000) *Millennials Rising: The Next Great Generation*, New York, NY: Vintage Books.

Huett, J., Moller, L., Foshay, W., and Coleman, C. (2008) "The evolution of distance education: Implications for instructional design on the potential of the web. Part 3: K-12," *TechTrends: Linking Research and Practice to Improve Learning*, 52(5), pp63–67.

ISTE (International Society for Technology in Education) (2009) *National Educational Technology Standards for Administrators (NETS.A)*, Eugene, OR: ISTE.

Jackson, L., Zhao, Y., Kolenic III, A., Fitzgerald, H., Harold, R., and Von Eye, A. (2008) "Race, gender, and information technology use: The new digital divide," *Cyber Psychology and Behavior*, 11(4), pp437–442.

Jonassen, D., Peck, K., and Wilson, B. (1998) *Learning with Technology in the Classroom: A Constructivist Perspective*, New York, NY: Merrill/Prentice Hall.

Johnson, L., Levine, A., and Smith, R. (2010) *The 2010 Horizon Report*, Austin, TX: New Media Consortium.

Kaiser Family Foundation (2009) *Generation M2: Media in the Lives of 8- to 18-Year Olds*, http://www.kff.org/entmedia/mh012010pkg.cfm.

Kowalski, T., Lasley, T., and Mahoney, J. (2008) *Data-Driven Decisions and School Leadership: Best Practices for School Improvement*, Boston, MA: Allyn and Bacon.

Larson, L., Miller, T., and Ribble, M. (2010) "Five considerations for digital age leaders: What principals and district administrators need to know about tech integration today," *Learning and Leading with Technology*, 37(4), pp12–15.

Lieberman, A. and Mace, D. (2009) "The role of 'accomplished teachers' in professional learning communities: Uncovering practice and enabling leadership," *Teachers and Teaching*, 15(4), pp459–470.

Looi, C., Chen, W., and Ng, F.-K. (2010) "Collaborative activities enabled by GroupScribbles (GS): An exploratory study of learning effectiveness," *Computers and Education*, 54(1), pp14–26.

Marzano, R. and Waters, T. (2009) *District Leadership that Works*, Bloomington, IN: Solution Tree.

McCoog, I. (2008) "Integrated instruction: Multiple intelligences and technology," *Clearing House*, 81(1), September/October, pp25–28.

McKenzie, K. (2007) "Digital divides: The implications for social inclusion," *Learning Disability Practice*, 10(6), July, pp16–21.

McKinsey and Company (2009) *The Economic Impact of the Achievement Gap in America's Schools*, New York, NY: McKinsey and Company, Social Sector Office.

Motavalli, J. (2007) "Talking computer trash," *E - The Environmental Magazine*, 18(1), January, pp59.

National Science Board (2010) *Science and Engineering Indicators 2010*, Arlington, VA: National Science Foundation, http://www.nsf.gov/statistics/seind10.

Nolan, J. and Hoover, L. (2011) *Teacher Supervision and Evaluation: Theory into Practice*, Hoboken, NJ: J. Wiley and Sons.

Obringer, S. and Coffey, K. (2007) "Cell phones in American high schools: A national survey," *Journal of Technology Studies*, 33(1/2), pp41–47.

O'Neil, H. and Perez, R. (2002) *Technology Applications in Education: A Learning View*, Mahwah, NJ: L. Erlbaum Publishers.

Ono, H. and Zavodny, M. (2008) "Immigrants, English ability, and the digital divide," *Social Forces*, 86(4), June, pp1455–1479.

Ormiston, M. (2011) *Creating a Digital Rich Classroom: Teaching and Learning in a Web 2.0 World*, Bloomington, IN: Solution Tree.

Papa, R. (ed) (2010) *Technology Leadership for School Improvement*, Thousand Oaks, CA: Sage Publications, Inc.

Picciano, A. (2011) *Educational Leadership and Planning for Technology*, 5th edition, Upper Saddle River, NJ: Pearson Education, Inc.

Pomona Unified School District Technology Use Plan (2010) Pomona, CA: Unpublished report.

Prensky, M. (2008) "Turning on the lights," *Educational Leadership*, 65(6), pp40–45.

Reeves, D. (ed) (2007) *Ahead of the Curve: The Power of Assessment to Transform Teaching and Learning*, Bloomington, IN: Solution Tree.

Roberson, S. and Roberson, R. (2009) "The role and practice of the principal in developing novice first-year teachers," *Clearing House*, 82(3), pp113–118.

Rock, M., Zigmund, N., Gregg, M., and Gable, R. (2011) "The power of virtual coaching," *Educational Leadership*, 69(2), pp42–47.

Roe, M. (2011) "Learning tools for innovation," *Leadership*, 40(4), pp32–38.

Roschelle, J. (2003) "Unlocking the learning value of wireless mobile devices," *Journal of Computer Assisted Learning*, 19(3), pp260–272.

Rosen, L. (2011) "Teaching the iGeneration," *Educational Leadership*, 68(5), pp10–15.

Ross, S., McDonald, A., Alberg, M., and McSparin-Gallagher, B. (2007) "Achievement and climate outcomes for the Knowledge is Power Program in an inner-city middle school," *Journal of Education for Students Placed at Risk*, 12(2), pp137–165.

Schrum, L. and Levin, B. (2009) *Leading 21st-Century Schools*, Thousand Oaks, CA: Corwin Press.

Schwartz, S. (2010) *Verizon Foundation Supports Innovative Technology Programs Preparing Underserved Students for Success in the 21st Century*, http://www.mouse.org/news-events/news/press-release/verizon-foundation-supports-innovative-technology-programs-preparing.

Sims, P., Springer, J., and Guthrie, J. (2006) *Successful Schools and Instructional Technology*, Old Tappan, NJ: Allyn and Bacon.

Snakenborg, J., Van Acker, R., and Gable, R. A. (2011) "Cyberbullying: Prevention and intervention to protect our children and youth," *Preventing School Failure*, 55(2), pp88–95.

Tadeja, C. (2010) "Blended learning environments: Visuals of context," *Scholar and Educator*, XXXI(1–2), pp22–29.

Tadeja, C. (2011a) *"The vital impact of technology, social media and volunteerism and philanthropy,"* in R. Vaisvilaite (ed) *Proceedings of the International Conference on Interdisciplinary Research at LCC International University*, LCC International University, Klaipeda, Lithuania: LCC University Press, pp41–48.

Tadeja, C. (2011b) *Blended Learning for the Developing Leader and Emerging Academic, Proceedings of the 2011 Navigating Your PATH Conference*, Toronto, Ontario, Canada.

Tadeja, C., Uribe, B., Garatli, A., and Martin, R. (2011a) "Strategic leadership," in T. Coleman (ed) *Leading with Social Intelligence*, Strategic Leadership, Dallas, TX: Chair Academy, pp44–51.

Tadeja, C., Uribe, B., Garatli, A., and Martin, R. (2011b) "Tomorrow's leaders," in V. Mladjenovic (ed) *The Emergence of Blended Learning Communities*, Bangkok, Thailand: Tomorrow People Organization, pp61–72.

Takahashi, D. (2007) "The brain as joystick: Start-up's headset lets emotions, expressions control gaming action," *San Jose Mercury News* (CA), retrieved from EBSCOhost, 13 March.

Twigg, C. A. (2005) "Redesign seminar: Getting started on course redesign," *The National Center for Academic Transformation*, www.thencat.org/Monographs/IncSuccess.pdf.

U.S. Department of Education (2010) *Transforming American Education: Learning Powered by Technology (NETP)*, Washington, DC: U.S. Department of Education, Office of Educational Technology.

Waters, J. (2011) "Move it or lose it: Cloud-based storage," *Education Digest*, 76(8), pp28–34.

Weiss, J. (2010) *U.S. Department of Education's Race to the Top Assessment Competition*, http://www2.ed.gov/programs/racetothetop-assessment/overview.pdf.

Williamson, J. and Redish, T. (2009) *ISTE's Technology Facilitation and Leadership Standards*, Eugene, OR: International Society for Technology in Education.

Wolk, R. (2007) "The real world," *Teacher Magazine*, 18(4), p. 54.

Young, P., Gyeong Mi, H., and Lee, R. (2011) "Blogging for informal learning: Analyzing bloggers' perceptions using learning perspective," *Journal of Educational Technology and Society*, 14(2), pp149–160.

Zhang, T., Mislevy, G., Haertel, H., Javitz, E., Murray, E., and Gravel, J. (2010) *A Design Pattern for a Spelling Assessment for Students with Disabilities (Assessment for Students with Disabilities Technical Report 2)*, Menlo Park, CA: SRI International, http://padi-se.sri.com/downloads/TR2_SpellingBee.pdf.

Web Resources

http://www.ala.org/aasl/guidelinesandstandards/guidelinesandstandards
This website represents the organization of the American Association of School Librarians whose main goal is to promote excellence in the school library field. Part of their mission is to provide leadership, connect learners with information, and prepare students for lifelong learning.

http://asapconnected.com/class-management-software.html
This website provides a wide range of web-based products and administrative tools, such as classroom management, community outreach, accounting, and event management.

http://www.blackboard.com/platforms/collaborate/overview.aspx
This website is online collaborative software that utilizes mobile learning devices to create virtual classrooms and meetings. Blackboard Collaborate combines the capabilities of other learning platforms, such as Wimba and Elluminate, and specifically gears its products and services to the educational community.

http://www.clayanimator.com

http://www.creativecommons.org

http://www.dailygalaxy.com/my_weblog/2009/07/augmented-reality-ar-overlaying-the-information-age-on-the-real-world.html

http://www.discoveryeducation.com/

http://docs.google.com
These tools are part of the Web 2.0 platform in which users consume media and use the web to access content and interact with the information. Although more of a marketing term, Web 2.0 tools are generally bi-directional uses of communication promoting user interaction and include the burgeoning growth and phenomenon of social networks and similar content types. Web 2.0 tools are generally accepted as the follow up to Web 1.0 tools, which were one way uses of accessing information.

http://www.dynamicgeometry.com

http://www.edibleapple.com/2009/08/25/first-augmented-reality-app-hits-the-iphone-app-store/

http://www.edmodo.com/

http://www.eff.org

http://www.exchange.smarttech.com/

http://www.freesound.org

http://www.freetech4teachers.com/

http://www.gaggle.net
This is a popular website that offers students the chance to utilize the web in a safe and effective manner, such as veiwing YouTube videos that have been filtered and deemed safe to watch.

http://groupscribbles.sri.com
This website enables both students and teachers to scribble contributions on electronic pages which are similar to a Post-it note. This visual representation of work done by students and teachers contributes to collaborative, adaptive learning.

http://www.imsglobal.org/

http://www.iport.iupui.edu/selfstudy/tl/milestones/uupp
This website gives access the Urban Universities Portfolio Project, a consortium of six urban public universities aimed at developing first-generation electronic institutional portfolios.

http://www.isafe.org
This website educates students on how to use the Internet in a safe and responsible manner through community outreach and Internet safety education.

http://www.istockphoto.com
This website is a repository of royalty-free images and media. This service promotes digital citizenship in the use of safe, legal, and ethical use of digital information.

http://www.khanacademy.com
This is the Khan Academy website, started by Salman Khan in 2008. It has instructional videos on topics ranging from language arts and calculus. The website now includes a focus on training materials and equipping and helping students succeed in learning.

http://www.learnar.org

http://learning.blogs.nytimes.com/

http://www.magnatune.com

http://www.mathforum.org
This website was formed by the Drexel University School of Education is an online resource that supports math learning and teaching. The website is designed by teachers, mathematicians, researchers, parents, citizens, and students who utilize the web to improve math learning.

http://www.ning.com

http://notebook.lausd.net/portal/page?_pageid=33,136640&_dad=ptl&_schema=ptl_ep

http://www.ode.state.oh.us/GD/Templates/Pages/ODE/ODEDefaultPage.aspx?page=1

http://piratepad.net

http://www.polldaddy.com

http://www.polleverywhere.com
This website provides a powerful learning tool and real-time poll gathering instrument using mobile devices or the Internet to cast votes on custom-made user-designed polls.

http://www.pppst.com/

http://www.pusd.org/education/components/docmgr/default.php?sectiondetailid=1245&fileite
m=561P

http://qrcode.kaywa.com/
This website generates quick response (QR) codes. QR codes are matrix barcodes that allows
users with QR readers to see, hear, or read information about said products.

http://www.sakaiproject.org

http://www.schoolsworld.tv
This is a multimedia platform providing innovative and informative content for users involved
with schools. Their content includes various media, including videos, games, and printed
materials. SchoolsWorld uses 25 years' of experience to connect users to relevant educational
materials.

http://www.sheeo.org
This website was developed by the State Higher Education Executive Officers and outlines some
of the challenges faced in staffing classrooms with quality teachers.

http://sliderocket.com
This website utilizes existing presentations to create multimedia presentations using the Internet
and mobile devices.

http://www.slideshare.net

http://www.stemedcoalition.org/
This website is designed to raise awareness in government and other organizations about the
critical role that STEM programs play in education.

http://www.sync.in

http://www.taskstream.com/

http://www.teachertube.com
This website is similar in format to the YouTube website. The main difference is that TeacherTube
has an educational focus, is specifically geared toward teaching and learning, and is generally a
place for instructional videos.

http://www.teachscape.com/products/walkthrough
This website provides three types of products: online learning content based on authentic
teaching methodologies; software tools for classroom observation and evaluation; and
professional support in implementing professional development. They offer a wide range of
services for educators that directly identifies teachers' needs and matches them directly with
products and services that supports their students' learning.

http://www.teamviewer.com/

http://www.ted.com

http://www.the-eg.com

http://www.udlcenter.org/aboutudl/udlguidelines
This website provides a framework in utilizing Universal Design for Learning. It also covers some of the major tenets for following the framework for UDL and can be incorporated into a classroom lesson.

http://www.uwplatt.edu/web/presentations/PennState/ar/index.html

http://www.WeCollaborate.com
This website has an independent user community that uses the tools of other learning platforms, such as Blackboard Collaborate, Elluminat, and Wimba. There are discussion groups, existing conversations, and a shared Web 2.0 lab that allows teachers or students to exchange resources.

http://www.wired.com/epicenter/2009/12/3d-maps-camera-phones-put-reality-in-augmented-reality/

Websites for Professional Organizations and Connected Learning

Adobe Connect web conferencing and learning module
www.adobe.com/products/adobeconnect.html

American Association of School Administrators
www.aasa.org

American Educational Research Association
www.aera.net

American Federation of Teachers
www.aft.org

Association for Educational Communications and Technology
www.aect.org

Association of Supervision and Curriculum Development
www.ascd.org

B2 Evolution
www.b2evolution.net:

Blogger
www.blogger.com

Blog Some
www.blogsome.com

Brookings Institution, Brown Center on Education Policy
www.brookings.org

Cato Institute
www.cato.org

Children's Online Privacy Protection Act
www.coppa.org

Citizens for Educational Freedom
www.educational-freedom.org

Commonwealth Educational Policy Institute
www.cepi.vcu.edu

Computer-Using Educators, Inc.
www.cue.org

Computerworld blog of emerging technologies
blogs.computerworld.com/emergingtech

Consortium for Policy Research in Education
www.cpre.org

Consortium of Advancing Intelligent Use of Information and Technology
www.educause.edu

Council of the Great City Schools
www.cgcs.org

cyber bullying prevention curriculum
www.nasponline.org/resources/cyberbullying/index.aspx

Education Commission of the States
www.ecs.org

Education Development Center
www.edc.org

Education Law Association
www.educationlaw.org

Educators' website for information technology
www2.edc.org/ewit

EdTechTalks discussions for teaching and learning
www.edtechtalks.wordpress.com

Electronic Portfolios
www.electronicportfolios.org

Elluminate Live! web conferencing service
www.elluminate.com

Facebook social networking service
www.facebook.com

Federal Trade Commission
www.ftc.gov

Google search engine
www.Google.com

Harvard Business Publishing for Educators
hbsp.harvard.edu

International Society for Technology in Education
www.iste.org

International Technology Education Association
www.iteaconnect.org

Layar augmented reality browser
www.layar.com

Live Journal
www.livejournal.com

Live videostreaming and lifecasting service
www.ustream.tv

Los Angeles County Office of Education
www.lacoe.edu

Moveable Type
www.movabletype.org

MySpace social networking
www.MySpace.com

National Association of Elementary School Principals
www.naesp.org

National Association of Secondary School Principals
www.nassp.org

National Center for Education Statistics
www.nces.ed.gov

National Charter School Clearinghouse
www.ncsc.info

National Clearinghouse for Educational Facilities
www.ncef.org

National Education Association
www.nea.org

National Education Technology Plan
www.ed.gov/technology/netp-2010

National Survey of Student Engagement
www.nsse.iub.edu

New Hampshire State Department of Education
www.ed.state.nh.us

Partnership for 21st Century Skills
www.p21.com

Polycom video and voice conferencing, data and web communications solutions
www.polycom.com

San Bernardino County Superintendent of Schools
www.sbcss.k12.ca.us

Science and learning with augmented reality
scimorph.greatfridays.com

The Seed Foundation
www.seedfoundation.com

Square Space Blogging Website
www.squarespace.com

Texas Computer Education Association
www.tcea.org

Text Pattern Blogging and Content Management System
www.textpattern.com

Twitter social network and blogging service
www.twitter.com

Type Pad Blogging Service
www.typepad.com

United States Department of Education
www.ed.gov

United States Department of Education Office of Educational Technology
www2.ed.gov/about/offices/list/os/technology/index.html

Web on-demand collaboration and video application tool
www.webex.com

Website communication platform
www.schoolfusion.com

Word Press blog tool and publishing platform
www.wordpress.org

Yahoo pulse blogging website
360.yahoo.com

ZD Net Emerging Technologies in Education
www.zdnet.com/blog/emergingtech

Index

acceptable use policy (AUP), 60, 93–4
accountability, demand for, 27
adaptive learning, 24–5
adequate yearly progress (AYP), 15, 92
administrators, school: adaptive learning
    technologies, 24, 25; communication tools for,
    52, 59–61; as instructional leaders, 13; National
    Education Technology Standards for *see*
    National Education Technology Standards for
    Administrators (NETS.A); supervision and
    professional development of teachers, 42, 48–9;
    as technology leaders, 45–6; technology
    resources for, 64; technology skills, need
    for, 18, 20; technology standards, revamping in
    2009, 1
Adobe Connect, 62
African Americans, 92
alternatives to traditional schools, technology
    enhanced, 4–5
American Association of School Librarians
    (AASL), 63
American School Board Journal, 96
Animoto (video presentation tool), 23
Arrow, Judith, 2
artificial intelligence theory, 24
Assessment Management Systems (AMS), 30
assessments, 27–33, 35; aggregated, 29;
    data-sharing, 33; embedded technologies, 13,
    32; feedback system, interconnected, 30;
    formative and summative, 28–32; Principled-
    Assessment Designs for Inquiry, 32–3;
    standardized tests, 4
ASSISTment tutoring system, Worcester County
    Public Schools (Massachusetts), 30
augmented reality technologies, 13, 24–5

Balanced Assessment Diet, 16, 35
Baton Rouge, Louisiana, 45
Berners-Lee, Tim, 43
Bill and Melinda Gates Foundation, 81, 91
Blackboard Collaborate, 61, 62
blogging, 60; as professional development, 45,
    46
Blue Valley School District, Kansas, 71
Bogler, R., 57
Bring Your Own Technology (BYOT), 72, 73, 77,
    78, 95

Broadband Data Improvement Act, 2008, 94
Brooks-Young, S., 7
"bug-in-the-ear" technologies, 40, 41

California State University Polytechnic
    Pomona, 63
Carnegie Foundation, 81
Carozza, William, 46, 51–3
cell phones, 18, 19, 40, 60, 95
certification of teachers, 63–4
Chamberlin, Steven, 46, 53
Children's Internet Protection Act (CIPA),
    94, 96, 97
Children's Online Privacy Protection Act, 97
Christensen, C.M., 32
Classroom 2.0, 61
classroom observation process, 41
classroom response systems, 28
Clay Animator (free software), 31
cloud computing, 56
Coalition of Essential Schools, 23
Coffey, K., 95
collaboration: communication tools, 61;
    cross-cultural and global, 97–8; data learning,
    collaborative, 17; partnerships, 22–3;
    technology for, 52, 61–3; visionary leadership, 6
Common Core Standards, 16, 91
communication tools, 52, 59–61
competency-based instruction, 4, 5, 11
compliance training, 93
computers, as interactive teaching devices, 24;
    see also digital age; Internet; Web 1.0 tools;
    Web 2.0 tools
Concordia University, Illinois, 44–5
conferences, as professional development, 47
Connaghan, Karen, 13–15
connected learning, 42, 43–4
copyright issues, 94–5
costs, procurement, 4
Creative Commons, 94, 95
Creighton, T., 92
culture-aware collaborative learning, 62
cyber-bullying, 96–7, 98
cyber-courses, 22
cyber-infrastructure, 53–7; interoperability
    standards, 56–7; new technology trends,
    54–6